Meals, Snacks, and Desserts for Gymnasts, Athletes, and Their Families (From a Gymnastics Nutrition Coach and her French Chef Hubby)

BETSY MCNALLY LAOUAR
MESS LAOUAR

Dedicated to Mess's mom, Meriem Laouar: The Magic Connection

MESS AND I DECIDED to collaborate on this book to merge our differing foods, cultures, and creativity to make something families would enjoy. However, along the way, we found out something amazing as our creating unraveled. There was a magic connection in all the foods we were using! The magic connection was Mess's mother, Meriem.

Many of the foods I wanted in this book were things Mess's mom had made for him as a boy in France or ones she'd cooked with decades ago, in Algeria. As I was selecting functional foods, beneficial for athletes, that were rich in nutrients, vitamins, minerals, healthy fats, and fiber, we started to make connections between the old world and the new.

You see, Mess was born and raised in France, but his parents were born in North Africa—Algeria, to be exact. Mess's dad arrived in France in 1957, and his mother later, in 1966. So his mother spent quite a bit of her life in Algeria. A lot of the foods and customs Mess adapted to his cuisine later in life were a combination of both French and Algerian foods. His mother, after moving to France, utilized her spices in traditional foods and incorporated them into French cuisine.

Much of North African food is actually very popular in France today, with delicious couscous, "merguez" (sausages) tajine, chorba, pastries and other delicacies originating from this area of the world. From lentils/chickpeas and grains to sardines, artichokes, dates, fresh fish, and olive oils, spices like cumin, turmeric, and parsley—which are all touted as health foods today—we came to realize that much of the healthy foods that athletes need are North African in nature.

Mess had seven sisters. He was the only boy. As a young boy, he would sit next to his mother in the kitchen and watch her slice, dice, stir and mix, prepare sauces and create all kinds of dishes, ranging from meat to fish, salads, bread, and soups. He would travel to the market with her and learned a lot as a child just watching her. (Yes, him alone—his sisters were off doing other things.) Later in life, as an adult, he would get specifics on the recipes that he'd observed her prepare, as a child. He was always fascinated with the kitchen, food markets, and putting meals together. Meriem instilled in him as a young child a respect for food that he carries with him still.

Mess's passion for his mother's cooking and its influence on him his whole life is bittersweet for me. Through it, I have been able to get to know a woman I never met. You see, she passed away in 2007, so I never had a chance to meet this amazing woman who bore seven daughters and one son—Mess.

She will never know the invaluable lessons she passed down to her son, then to me, and now to you....

CONTENTS

Have an open mind, an open palette, and know this comes from our hearts and our kitchen.

PREFACE AND HOW TO USE THIS BOOK

BEFORE YOU READ this book, we want to tell you about the products we used for the recipes. We used particular molds, mixing machines, utensils, and products to make our delicious creations.

You can find these products and utensils on Betsy's website home page, www.betsymcnally.com, in the Books and Online Store Tab. Please then search under Betsy's Equipment Recommendations and Cooking Tools.

You may feel free to use your own utensils and products, too, but these are what we used and what worked best for us. From electric mixers to blenders, strainers, graters, and molds, we feature everything you'll need to make the recipes in this book. Be sure to read the beginning of each recipe, to make sure you have all the required tools before you start your cooking.

We did our best to provide you with all of the nutritional content, however we also want to stress that we do *not* recommend getting caught up on the numbers! We truly believe in eating everything in moderation or until filling your intuitive need. We do not believe in over-calculating macronutrients, calories, etc. We promote balance, and Betsy has found that, over twenty years of serving clients, this works best for overall health and sanity!

Also, woven throughout this book are Betsy's ideas on nutrition for families and athletes, French quotes, and thoughts from Mess, as well as educational articles, tips, and advice for gymnasts, with the last section of the book dedicated to gymnasts specifically. Betsy includes information from research-backed presentations during her Certification in Sports

Nutrition and Performance through Educational Fitness Solutions and Chicago State University, including courses in Functional Foods, Weight Management and Nutrition in the Lifecycle, Introduction to Sports Nutrition and Performance, and Public Nutrition and Wellness Education.

Another important note: we did *not* have our recipe photos retouched. We had the option of doing that, but we wanted to present the food in its natural state. We used an iPhone to take most of the pictures, except for the ones of Betsy and Mess in the kitchen. We wanted to clean up for you guys!

We hope you use this book as both a recipe book and a resource for your athletes.

To your health!

Betsy & Mess

Follow us on Instagram @GYMNACHEF!

@betsy_mcnally_laouar

ଔଔଔଔ

"Les rires éclatent mieux lorsque la nourriture est bonne."

(Laughs burst better when the food is GOOD)

—Irish Proverb

Mess's Thoughts:

Good food brings good laughter with friends and family...

INTRODUCTION

By Betsy McNally Laouar

SO, YOU PROBABLY think you just picked up a cookbook for gymnasts, athletes, and their families. Well, you did, but this book is way more than that...!

You just picked up a love story, a resource for gymnasts, *and* an educational book, all in one complete package.

To begin, this is a love story about food and a passion for health with, at its center, two people who are spiritually and forever bonded by both.

We are the perfect marriage of a French Chef and a Nutrition Coach. We have the same mission: To help families, gymnasts, and athletes eat clean foods that are homemade, non-processed, healthy, and delicious.

You may be asking, "Is that even possible?" In a word, *YES*!

Before we go any further, please know this is *not* in any way, shape, or form a Diet Book! It is a resource for families who want to cook clean, healthy foods. The recipes are interspersed with my experiences working with athletes, plus educational tools and tips and articles along the way.

Both my husband and I are focused on whole foods and balance. Although there are a few gluten-free, vegetarian, and vegan items in the book, the recipes here are not targeted toward those who have restrictions or allergies, because that is not our main focus.

We, ourselves, have a son, Ayden, who suffers from fruit allergies and another son, Lenny, who has non-verbal autism and has had eating aversions since birth. He literally did not eat solid food until he was three years old, only cookies, and he has struggled his entire life with food.

We live this daily battle ourselves, and so we are empathetic toward families who struggle with severe allergies. In the future, we hope to create another book that deals with these areas specifically, so stay tuned.

This book comes from our heart and our kitchen. We are sharing our ideas in hopes that athletes and their parents will cook together, discover and find new combinations of healthy foods, and perhaps re-establish eating together, making meals together, sitting down, and enjoying the beauty of food. We also wanted to help move our readers out of their comfort zone and possibly try some new foods or combinations of foods.

We started with this basic book, which will give families healthy alternatives to some old favorites, in order to get athletes eating more green, nutrient-dense foods. These are foods that will energize and help with inflammation and immunity. Foods rich in the omega-3s, antioxidants, vitamins, minerals, complex carbs, and whole grains that help athletes reach their potential.

We also wanted to combine my husband's rich knowledge and background in French food with my specialization in healthy foods for athletes.

In this book, I want to share the vast knowledge I have accrued over the years, working with gymnasts specifically, through my camps, one-on-one training, and nutrition coaching. That is why the second part of the book is dedicated to education for athletes and their families. I feel very honored and proud to say I have yet to see a book specifically written for gymnasts and nutrition. If there is one, forgive me! I would venture to say, though, it more than likely will not include recipes created by a French chef and his wife.

The recipes in GymnaChef are beautiful creations, and we use ingredients that, as a married couple, we married together. We did not focus on calories, macronutrients, or calculating ratios of foods. Although we do include a light nutritional breakdown, if you are looking for a diet book, again, this isn't it.

This book is an introduction to families for how to make dishes that are delicious and have functional components to them. We believe, if we can transition families away from fast food and processed foods and toward eating in a cleaner, more balanced way, then we are helping our culture get healthier, stave off heart disease and high blood pressure, and increase immunity.

One of our other goals is to decrease the alarming rate of obesity and increase education on whole foods. This is a back-to-basics-type book. It's not a quick-fix book. It's not a "lose weight" book.

It's a cookbook filled with beautiful, creative ideas that we are both proud of and want to share with you and your family.

That being said...

My husband and I don't agree a lot—LOL—and that is what makes our story magical. That is what actually makes our relationship work. This feisty pair can make some magic in the kitchen, though!

If you follow us on social media, you know we are the perfect storm of passion, humor, energy, intensity, and stubbornness.

We don't always agree on the same "way to go" or even use the same ingredients in our own cooking. I had to work really hard to convince my husband to try some of my ideas, specifically using more greens, lean proteins, healthy fats, whole grains, and seeds.

He had to really try to convince me about some of his cheeses, sugars, creams, and breads. (He did, by the way!)

I am a pescatarian (fish and veggies) girl, and my husband is a big meat and bread eater. He was born and raised in Alsace, France, just west of the German border. I grew up in the suburban Midwest of America, eating processed, traditional American foods.

I am also a recovered binge eater, and if you have followed my story, you know I wrote a book called *Binges and Balance Beams,* about my life as a young gymnast who was told by a coach I was too heavy to do gymnastics. That one comment led me down a road to obsessive behavior with food and exercise.

My husband, on the other hand, grew up with a rich experience of food, eating wholesome, functional foods along with lots of croissants, breads, and chocolate. (Well, he is French, of course!) He had the best of *all* worlds, from fresh fish, beef, fruits, and vegetables, legumes, and oils to sweet pastries, chocolates, and the delicacies of France. But, overall, he ate healthy and everything in moderation.

So, how did we come together to make this lovely book? Our love story begins like this...

I met Mess in Paris and had no idea what I would be in for. We stayed in touch online for many months before we met, but I had no idea that the romantic ideals of French life would permeate into my own world.

I was attracted to his fierce spirit, his accent, and the mystique of his living in France. I had always been captivated with Paris and had visited before we met. I took many years of French in high school and college, so I had a good foundation of the language. Speaking with a French person was exciting.

I also knew he was a chef and loved food. I had never met a man who knew so much about cooking and ingredients and who actually loved to cook for me. I found it charming, refreshing, and sexy.

Not only that, but the foods he made tasted so good, I couldn't resist trying them. I struggled at first, because I was so conscious of "dieting" and being fit that I thought his food would make me fat.

In actuality, when I moved to France, I lost nine pounds within the first month and a half. How was I drinking wine, eating cheese, bread, and chocolate, and losing weight? That is another book in itself... But, in short, he changed my whole concept of the word "diet."

When I met Mess, I was just overcoming binge-eating disorder and a divorce. As a binge eater and professional bodybuilder, fitness coach, and gymnastics coach, I was at a point in my life when I wanted to explore other foods than just diet foods.

I had been a big restricter then a binger for most of my thirties, when I was competing in fitness competitions, where my body fat would go lower than ten percent and then skyrocket to over twenty-eight percent. When we got married and I moved to France, I learned about whole foods and eating rich ingredients like butter, chocolate, and bread in moderation. I learned about North African cuisine, as both of Mess's parents originated from Algeria. I learned about the many different types of cheese, cream, and grains, as well as the varieties of seafood and fruit that are available from North Africa and the Mediterranean.

The grocery stores in France were amazing to me. I couldn't believe the rows and rows and rows of cheese, plus the many different forms of dairy products, specifically all the different consistencies of creams and cheeses.

I never knew there were so many different forms of dairy! I stood in awe of French grocery stores. The fresh fruits and vegetables, the meat selection and fruits of the sea: it was all beautiful.

I also learned about different grains, different combinations of foods, and different ways of preparation. I started to open my mind to eating like the French. I felt, as an American, I had been cheated out of so many options!

I also discovered that so much of the food in Europe is hormone- and pesticide-free, labeled "bio" or what we call organic. My stomach issues dissipated, and I felt more energized and alive when I lived in France. You could taste the freshness in all of the products, even the ones that appeared to be processed.

You see, France introduced me to forbidden foods that I thought would make me fat. I saw the French people eating chocolate and cheese and wondered, why the hell are we Americans overweight, obese, and confused about food? And the French are over here with their baguettes and pastries, looking pretty fit!

You may see some of the ingredients in this book and say, "Hey! I thought butter was fattening! Why does Betsy have butter, cream, and chocolate in this book?" Well, in fact, although these foods may be fattening in excess, in moderation they are not. And that is the message that Mess and I would like to send you, our readers.

Americans have become fearful of real whole foods, and that is where we have gone wrong, replacing real "forbidden" foods with synthetic sugar alcohols or going on diets that encourage eating an abundance of one food group and eliminating another. (For instance, the Atkins or Keto diets.) Eat more fat and less carbs and sugar and lose weight? No, thank you.

Everyone is always looking for the next quick fix when in actuality the truth is, if you eat everything in moderation and eat functional foods that can help you, you most likely will feel amazing.

I have come to realize, after traveling to *hundreds* of cities all over the country with my nutrition and fitness camp (Betsy Bootcamps), whether it's small-town Tupelo, Mississippi or big-city New York, most Americans are so caught up with what *not* to eat that they are substituting those foods with an excess amounts of other foods and eating out of balance.

Replacing one food with another and restricting doesn't work. The only thing, over time, that has proven to work is balance and the appropriate caloric intake. If we could just focus on that, being satisfied with enjoying the foods we like (even chocolate) in moderation, then we will be okay... But, until we change our extreme ways, I believe Americans are going to be fighting a lot of battles with food addiction and disease.

Whether it's the Keto diet, the low-carb diet, the low-fat diet, a fasting regime—diets *don't* work, long term. Lifestyle changes *do*.

One challenge I've tried to help Mess understand is that Americans, unlike the French, don't understand moderation. A lot of French foods include very rich and calorie-dense ingredients like cream, cheese, butter, chocolate, and sauces. But the French can stop at one serving, where Americans are used to a "supersized" portion.

Throughout these recipes, I wanted to focus on using alternative ingredients, like coconut oil and whole grains, whereas Mess is a baguette kind of guy! It's been wonderful for us to share our ideas, because he has introduced me to new techniques and I have taught him how to implement new foods (like whole grains, sweet potatoes, and Ezekiel breads) that the French don't incorporate often in their diets. (Do you know how difficult it was for me to find sweet potatoes in France?)

I think you will find we have done a great job combining our forces to create homemade, functional recipes in the tastiest way possible without going overboard on the butter and cream. (Sweet potato crème Brûlée and coconut cordon bleu are both alternatives to richer recipes.)

I love that Mess grew up eating fresh, whole, and very functional foods. When I say functional, I mean foods that offer added benefits, with extra nutrients, vitamins, and minerals that can actually help the body through immunity, inflammation, digestion, heart health, or additional antioxidants.

Mess's mom Meriem prepared his lunch every day and dinners, as well. They ate together, and even today, Mess struggles with the lack of family togetherness while dining that he sees here in America. For him growing up, eating was an experience, a time to talk, get caught up, and also enjoy and savor the amazing blessings of the day.

I've learned a lot from my husband, and we have incorporated a lot of these French values into our kitchen. I started to take some of his ideas, and he started taking my ideas. That is how this beautiful book came about. It was a no-brainer: how could a French chef and his nutritionist wife *not* write a book? Well, here we are.

It has also helped me in my nutrition business, as I work specifically with gymnasts, giving them recommendations for their nutrition plans. I have been able to take my ideas and splash some amazing techniques, spices, and fun into some pretty boring dishes.

Please know, writing this book has not been easy. The French language has a different syntax or word order. So, when Mess was explaining how to make his food, I had to write things down in his language. Then, I had to go back and edit every single word. We also had to repeat recipes several times over and over, to get the outcomes perfect for you.

We also had many arguments. Have you ever argued with a French person? *LOL*! It's not easy, but we made it through and had a blast, too. We spent many hours dancing to hip hop and Kool and the Gang, fighting over ingredients and me telling him, "More vegetables! More green!!" Music in the kitchen is essential. Mess is a huge fan of the funky music of the seventies and eighties, as am I. So, our kitchen sounds good, smells good, and tastes good...!

Of course, as a gymnastics coach and nutritionist, my focus is to give my clients/athletes functional foods that are going to help them get stronger, have more energy, and heal. Foods that help with inflammation, hormonal changes, and sleep. I have thought deeply on every single recipe in this book, and I can assure you, the ingredients are helpful to athletes: whether they are gymnasts, soccer players, dancers, or football players, there is something for everyone in this book.

Finally, one of the *biggest* reasons we wrote this book is because, in our opinion and perhaps in the opinions of others, Americans are desperately caught up in a fast-food lifestyle.

Americans, generally speaking, are overeating processed and fast foods because we don't have the time or make the time to put food as a priority. Our priorities, in addition to our education and careers, include extra-curricular activities for our children, such as multiple sports, clubs, hobbies, lessons, plus travel and family obligations. The question seems to be, "How fast we can get somewhere?"

We need to slow down, because the average American family is taking on way too much and food is taking a back seat. Grab-and-go and drive-thrus, ordering in, and going out are the norm. This is setting our families up for unhealthy eating habits, disease, and, if you have kids participating in sports, lack of performance.

Oftentimes, I see kids in the gym coming into practice tired, lethargic, or moody. Could it be the processed foods they are putting into their body? Could it be the lack of nutrient-dense, functional foods loaded with magnesium, potassium, calcium, protein, and omega-3s? There are foods that help with inflammation, and there are foods that make inflammation worse. These kids are already tired and sore; by adding "fuel to the fire" with processed sugars, athletes are suffering at a cellular level. A lot of times, they simply aren't educated about food. That is why I love my job, because I am able to share different ideas and recipes, including the foods in this book.

Parents are spending thousands of dollars and countless hours in the gym, paying for leotards, competition travel, and tuition, while fueling their kids on protein bars and Lunchables. And we wonder why the kids are tired, have broken bones and injuries, and are sore all the time. Processed foods lead to inflammation, fatigue, bloating, and sometimes lowered mood. That is why this book is loaded with serotonin-boosting foods, energy-enhancing foods, and water-dense foods.

Over time, as we have lived with each other and started our own family together, Mess and I now realize we eat a lot differently. However, we both agree that whole, fresh foods are the most important thing to us and what we feed our kids. We do not want to be a part of this fast-food lifestyle. Making time to eat together is so important for our family. We are not pointing fingers. In fact, we are all guilty of falling in the trap of fast-and-quick-food options. However, there comes a time when we all must take responsibility for the food we put in our bodies.

We agree we want our children to eat a balance of foods, including healthy fats, proteins, full-fat cheese, organic dairy, an array of fruits and vegetables, plus treats like dark chocolate and even cookies and pizza. We believe in homemade goodness. We believe in everything in moderation and balance. And we truly hope you can adopt this with your family and your athletes.

One last thing. This book also includes tons of articles I have written on nutrition. They are woven in throughout. Please make it a priority to read these (not just the recipes), as there are countless tips, information, and ideas for feeding the gymnast.

I can't tell you how many times I get asked questions about nutrition for gymnasts. I have dedicated my life to helping the gymnast. I understand their special food needs and have worked one-on-one with some of the top gymnasts in the world around their nutrition. Try it out. I think you will find it works, when applied.

Now to the good stuff... As you are cooking these foods, we hope you think about our story, about France, about functional food, and about all of the amazing nutrients you will be putting into your body. AND, put on a little Kool and The Gang, and *Celebrate* these beautiful creations. We will be there with you.

Me and Mess in France

PART ONE

RECIPES, BETSY'S THOUGHTS & QUOTES FROM THE CHEF

Betsy's Thoughts: Why I've Dedicated My Life to Nutrition for Gymnasts

I WAS A LEVEL-10 gymnast, and I struggled throughout my career with injuries and being out of shape. I had no idea how to fuel my body or prevent injury, and I had very low self-esteem due to several comments made by a coach, who made me believe I wasn't fit enough to do gymnastics.

As many of you know, I have dedicated my life to working with gymnasts. I currently travel the country and world with my Betsy Bootcamps, teaching nutrition, fitness, and body image to gymnasts and parents.

Gymnastics is a special sport that takes a lot of discipline, strength, flexibility, and mental training. For many years now, I've been studying how food directly affects brain functioning, mood, and performance in this sport.

I find gymnastics to be one of the most challenging sports due to the complexity of the technical shaping, corrections given by coaches, and the complete accuracy with which a gymnast must perform. Technical perfection is the end goal of each event in this sport.

How many sports do you know where you have to make corrections while spinning upside down, holding multiple tight shapes through very fast speeds?

How many sports do you know where you have to also wear a leotard and jump around for four to six hours, even if you are feeling bloated, tired, not great about the way you look, or going through puberty?

Many gymnasts, as young children, do not think about that when they are under the age of twelve. Then, *bam!* Puberty hits, and bodies change, hormones change, and it becomes a different sport entirely for so many different reasons.

I was one of those kids, and I never had help when this happened…

Developing body strength, body tension, endurance, and flexibility are all part of this sport. All of these things are truly dependent on the foods you put into your body.

There are foods that will make you jump higher. There are foods that will make you tired. There are foods that will enhance your memory and mood, and there are foods that will deplete your energy and make your thoughts cloudy.

Food can directly affect how a gymnast feels about herself, whether it's through the way she looks, how high she's jumping, or how much energy she has throughout practice.

Nutrition is the Fifth Event of gymnastics. Somebody told me a couple of years ago that a coach already coined this phrase "The Fifth Event" and even wrote a book about it. Great minds must think alike, because I had never heard of this. Forgive me if this is something that has already been stated in the gymnastics community.

My thoughts are that gymnastics has four events: Vault, Bars, Beam, and Floor, and the Fifth Event is Nutrition. (I would agree that Mental Training should also be an event!)

A lot of gymnasts practice vault, bars, beam, and floor, but how many people actually practice nutrition? Based on what I see in the gyms I come into contact with, there are some, but far fewer than I would like to report.

Several years ago, I started traveling to gyms to explain the effects of nutrition on the gymnast. What I've come to find is gymnastics is unlike any other sport on the planet. There are so many stigmas surrounding weight, body image, and physical appearance. This is tricky, a dangerous and sensitive topic, one that is difficult to broach or even discuss without someone claiming you are body-shaming their athlete or child...

So many parents have contacted me for my nutrition programs during this very sensitive time....

This is one of the biggest issues I've had to face as a nutritionist in the sport. As a former gymnast and competitive bodybuilder, I myself have finally found balance in my own personal life and have helped others to achieve this. If I can share my experiences and wisdom with others through training and nutrition programs, I'm hoping this book will reach even a bigger audience. And also help those athletes whose bodies are changing and need proper education.

Many times, people ask me how to handle this very delicate situation. If you have an athlete who is going through body changes and is also doing gymnastics, you know what I'm talking about.

This is the reason why I wrote my first book, *Binges and Balance Beams.* As an athlete, I was told that I was too heavy to do the sport. This, of course, shattered my world, gave me low self-esteem, and affected me most of my teenage and adult life.

If I would've had just one person tell me what to eat, when to eat, how to eat, and why I need to eat a certain way, I truly believe my gymnastics experience and career would've been completely different.

I feel it's my responsibility to get in front of kids before they have the same issues I had. I struggled with my weight for many years, and I became obsessed with my body, I started exercising obsessively, and I took it to the next level. So far that I actually became a professional bodybuilder, just to show my coaches how strong and fit I could really be.

However, after achieving professional status in bodybuilding, I realized my motive for getting in superior shape was not based on a positive experience. It was based on a negative experience I had as a child, going through puberty. I was using my anger to fulfill my self-worth.

I didn't understand this until later on, after overcoming binge eating disorder and wrapping my head around the fact that most of the issues in my life had to do with the fact that I'd had problems with the way my body looked.

I never want another gymnast or athlete to have to deal with this part of the sport.

So, that is why I've dedicated all of my time, effort, and resources to my Betsy Bootcamps and nutritional and fitness education for athletes. Betsy Bootcamp has reached thousands of gymnasts all over the country. What I love about my camp is the ability to go into a gym with great energy and tell and teach these girls about nutrition. A lot of them don't know the first thing about nutrition, because many of them come from the type of families I spoke of in the introduction, who are living a fast-food lifestyle.

Many don't understand the direct connection between their energy level and their performance. And how could they? We live in such a fast-paced world, filled with fast-food and quick snacks, where our priorities are on the sports themselves, but not the nutrition that goes into powering the body. Education is the only way to truly correct this problem.

So, that is it. That is my mission. To touch as many gymnasts' lives as I can with my balanced-eating approach that teaches functional and clean eating approach, and in turn touch their families' lives, as well. If you think Betsy Bootcamp may need to come to your gym, check me out www.betsymcnally.com. I will gladly come to speak with your families and athletes!

Strong Gymnasts

GREAT-START BREAKFASTS

Betsy's Apple Pie Morning Shake

Most kids *LOVE* apple pie. This recipe came as a mistake. I had ground up oatmeal to make oat powder for another recipe and left some residue in the Bullet blender before making a protein shake. I was surprised by the texture, so I started to experiment more. What I found was a full-meal experience!

I love this shake for breakfast, because it contains all of the protein, vitamins, and minerals plus healthy fiber that an athlete needs to power through the first part of their day and then some! It is a very textured shake, so be aware of that. If your kid loves apple pie and oatmeal, they will love this! You can use an apple corer. (The utensil is on our shopping list, if you don't have one.)

One of the most perfect foods for any athlete is oats. Oats are packed with vitamins, minerals, soluble and insoluble fiber, and protein, and they will give sustained energy to a long workout. I believe oatmeal is the most perfect breakfast food because it can be used in so many ways: in shakes, pancakes, eaten dry in yogurt, or with water or your favorite almond milk.

Tools

* You need a blender, but we recommend the Nutri Bullet (also in our store, www.betsymcnally.com)
* Apple corer (in our store, not mandatory)

Makes Two Servings

Nutrition

Calories Per Serving: 298
Total Fat: 4.5g
Sodium: 284 mg
Total Carbohydrate: 42.2 g
Sugars: 16.3 g
Protein: 23.5 g

Ingredients

1/2 cup dry oatmeal

1 scoop vanilla protein

1 apple, cored

1 teaspoon cinnamon

2 cups ice

1 cup almond milk

Steps

1. Core your apple.
2. Discard the center and add the apple (sliced), along with all ingredients to your Nutri Bullet or blender and mix well.
3. Add a little water if you want a thinner shake.
4. Blend very well and enjoy!

Quick Mug Omelet

Quick morning breakfasts are always a hot topic with my clients! This is a great, quick breakfast option, however *please* remember to take out the eggs every thirty seconds, or you will have an egg explosion party!

It may take a few times for you to get it just right, but it will be worth it when you do! The preparation of this meal must be followed exactly as written!

Also, YES there is heavy cream in here! It's ok! Athletes need to eat FAT in moderation, and balance! I truly believe that and so does Mess! I do recommend eating organic dairy when and if possible.

You will need a microwave safe mug for this recipe (we have included these in our store too)

I love eggs for athletes because of their protein-rich makeup and significant amount of vitamin B! Excellent for energy, as well full of protein!

Tools

* You need a microwave safe mug for this recipe (you can find in our store, www.betsymcnally.com)

Makes one serving

Nutrition

Calories Per Serving: 385
Sodium: 525 mg
Fat: 15 g
Sugar: 1.4 g
Carbohydrate: 5.7
Protein: 21.2

Ingredients

1/2 cup chopped spinach

1 tablespoon goat cheese

2 eggs

Sprinkle salt

Pepper **to taste**

1 tablespoon heavy cream (organic recommended)

1/2 tablespoon flour

1/2 tablespoon olive oil

Steps

1. Place the salt, spinach, and 2 eggs in a coffee mug.
2. Then add all ingredients except goat cheese and whisk with a fork.
3. Next add the goat cheese, after it's whisked.
4. Cover the mug with a plate. *This is important.*
5. Cook for 30 seconds in the microwave.
6. Stop to check and make sure it doesn't explode or isn't cooking too fast.
7. Place back in microwave for another 30 seconds.
8. Check again and add another 30 seconds.

9. Place a spoon in the center to see how well it is cooking. Then, one more time, cook for 30 seconds.

The eggs should be firm and cooked through but not rubbery. Check by pushing down with a fork to make sure it's cooked thoroughly.

Make sure you wait for it to cool a bit when it first comes out! And be certain your mug is microwave-safe for cooking and doesn't get too hot. Happy Breakfast!

Quinoa and Fruit Salad

Mess came up with this delicious side dish/breakfast treat. I wanted something that involved quinoa, but in a "sweet way." Quinoa is loaded with protein, vitamins, minerals, and fiber and is somewhat nutty in flavor. I wanted to pair a sweet partner with this savory, nutty taste. The antioxidant-rich berries and kiwi will start any athlete's day right! You can also serve this as a side dish to a savory chicken, meat, or fish dinner, for a sweet pairing.

This recipe is also influenced by French summer foods. The French enjoy eating grains with fruits in the south of France. This dish was inspired by the summers Mess spent in south France.

Tools

* ✳ You need a blender or Nutri Bullet for this recipe. (In our store, www.betsymcnally.com)

Prep Time: 1 hour (we recommend you make the day before and serve in the morning)

Serves 4

Nutrition

Calories Per Serving: 186.5
Sodium: 15 mg
Fat: 8g
Sugar: 9.5
Carbohydrate: 25
Proteins: 8g

Ingredients:

Sauce

6 strawberries

1/2 cup coconut milk

2 tablespoons brown sugar

3 fresh mint leaves

Salad:

1/2 cup blueberries

1/2 cup raspberries

2 kiwis

1-1/2 cup quinoa

1-1/2 cup water

1 teaspoon brown sugar

Optional honey

Steps

1. If your quinoa is not pre-rinsed, rinse your quinoa with cold water in a fine, mesh strainer. Let dry well. (Most of the time quinoa is pre-rinsed, but just in case it isn't.)
2. Over medium heat, toast the quinoa in a pan for 3 minutes.
3. Remove from heat and add the water. Then place it back on the heat. Cook over medium heat for 20 minutes, turning and watching every few minutes.
4. Next, place the finished grains in a mixing bowl and let sit for one hour in the refrigerator, covered with plastic wrap.
5. While cooling, make the sauce. Put the strawberries, coconut milk, mint and brown sugar in a blender or bullet.

6. Mix for 30 seconds. Then place in the refrigerator.
7. After an hour, remove quinoa and place the blueberries and raspberries on top.
8. Pour the sauce on top.
9. Slice the kiwis, and place them on the side or on top.
10. Optional: if you would like it a little sweeter, add a drizzle of honey.

Yummy and powerful!

Gymnast Dream Dark Chocolate Protein Pancakes

As a competitive bodybuilder, my diet would get pretty bland. I got very tired of eating oatmeal and egg whites, so I started to play around with different combinations of oats, eggs, and proteins, and making different patties and pancakes. Somewhere along the line, I came up with this one, and I have never looked back.

For this recipe, I have toyed with many versions. Your choice of products (specifically the protein used) will make a difference. If you would like thicker pancakes, add less or more liquid or even water. Again, feel free to experiment a bit with exact liquid amounts. Depending on the fat content of your protein powder, there will be differences in consistency in general. Be open to the first few batches you make!

I love this recipe because of the high protein and fiber content. It has healthy fat for brain function, and the dark cocoa adds a potent antioxidant and serotonin boost! It's a great Sunday Funday Treat or a morning meal that will give you energy until lunch. You can also freeze them and pop them in the microwave or in a pan for a quick snack!

Makes 2 Servings

Nutrition:

Calories Per Serving: 265
Sodium 295 mg
Fat 12.5 g
Sugar 10g
Carbohydrate 27g
Protein 25.3

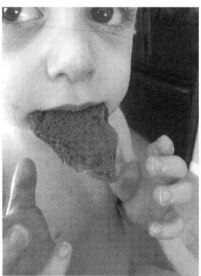

Even our son Ayden likes the dark-chocolate protein pancake!

Ingredients:

1 tablespoon coconut oil

4 egg whites

1 whole egg

1/4 cup dry oatmeal

1/4 cup almond flour

1 cup almond milk (more or less depending on preferred texture)

1 scoop protein powder

1 tablespoon of dark cocoa powder

1 teaspoon cinnamon

1 tablespoon coconut sugar

A pinch of baking powder (I mean really tiny!)

Steps

1. Add eggs and almond milk to a large mixing bowl and beat well.
2. Then add the dry oats and almond flour, and baking powder. Mix well. Add in the protein powder. If more almond milk or water is needed, add now for your desired consistency.
3. Last, add in the cocoa powder and mix well.
4. On a skillet, heat the coconut oil. It will melt quickly!
5. Using a measuring cup, pour out desired amount of batter into the skillet, and cook your pancakes! You can make many small ones or a couple large ones!
6. Top with cinnamon and coconut sugar and a little more coconut oil, if you like. This is a breakfast you can eat in the car, on the go, or pop in the microwave after freezing! YUM!

Lime-Whipped Greek Yogurt with Pomegranate Crunch

This recipe is not only loaded with antioxidants, protein, probiotics, and vitamin C, but it is also a colorful snack I like to use around Christmas because of its green and red color and seasonal relevance. Pomegranates are in season during the holidays, so take advantage of them with this delicious recipe.

Greek yogurt is packed with protein and probiotics—two gymnast and athlete essentials for proper gut functioning and muscle repair. The yogurt is infused with delicious immunity-boosting lime skin and juice. This food is rich in vitamin C, too, which will help stave off sickness during the holiday months. The yogurt is topped with powerful antioxidant- and energy-enhancing pomegranates and metabolic-boosting cinnamon! Your athlete will love this as a breakfast or a pre-/post-workout snack Oh, and did I mention the lovely crunch of the rice cake? It makes the snack complete!

Tools:

* You need a grater for the lime (Find in our store, www.betsymcnally.com)
* A bowl or glass that can fit a rice cake inside.
* A Kitchen Aide or regular whisk (Kitchen Aide also in our store; highly recommended for great whipped texture)

Serves 2-4

Nutrition

Calories Per Serving: 325
Sodium: 133mg
Fat: 5g
Sugar: 22 g
Carbohydrate: 49.g
Protein 25g

Ingredients

2 cups of 2% FAGE Greek yogurt, plain flavor

1 organic lime

1 pomegranate

1 tablespoons honey

1/2 teaspoon cinnamon

2-4 organic rice cakes (we like Lundberg Farms Organic Brands)

Steps

1. Grate the skin of your whole organic lime (if not organic, be sure to wash very, very well) with a grater into a small prep bowl. Save the rest of the lime for its juice.
2. Place the two cups of Greek yogurt in a mixing bowl.
3. Cut your lime in half and squeeze one of the lime halves into the yogurt. Mix in the grated skin.
4. Add the honey and mix well for three minutes with a whisk or a Kitchen Aide Electric mixer whisk attachment. Whisk.
5. Add the cinnamon and continue to mix until thoroughly blended.
6. Cut open your pomegranate and pull apart the skin. Remove **3 tablespoons** of seeds. Be sure to peel evenly and discard the skin parts.

7. Put a rice cake on your bowl or mug.
8. Top it with **1/3 to 1/2 cup** of the mixture.
9. Top with **3 tablespoons** of pomegranate seeds and some extra lime grates, if you like.
10. We also like to take another rice cake, crumble it, and add some crumbles to the top with an extra dash of cinnamon. Bon Breakfast!

Mess's Berry Delicious Breakfast Waffle

Loaded with vitamin C, antioxidants, protein, fiber, healthy fat, and delicious complex carbs, you can't beat this morning waffle. This is also one of Betsy's favorite recipes for her gymnasts—she uses it frequently on their meal programs.

One of the most powerful foods on the planet is berries. Specifically, blueberries, which are packed with brain-enhancing compounds that have been clinically proven to help memory and cognitive response. Berries are also rich in anti-oxidant and anti-inflammatory properties. Not only that, but they are tasty and kids *love* them.

You won't go wrong with this waffle! Make a batch on Sunday and freeze them for the week for pre-workout snacks. Or enjoy them on the weekends together for brunch. As stated before, *WE* have already tried this recipe with several of our gymnast clients and the grade is an A+!

Tools

* A Nutri Bullet
* A waffle iron (both in our store, www.betsymcnally.com)

Serves 2

Nutrition

Calories per serving: 350
Sodium: 81 mg
Fat: 21.9g
Sugar: 5.2g
Carbohydrate: 31.8g
Protein: 13 g

Ingredients:

1 **cup** rolled oats

2 eggs

1/4 **cup** almond flour

1/4 **cup** blueberries

4 large strawberries

1 **tablespoon** coconut oil

1/4 **cup** almond milk

1 **tablespoon** raw turbinado sugar

1 **tablespoon** chia seeds

Steps

1. Preheat waffle iron. (You will not need any precooking spray, as the coconut oil will provide that.)
2. Place everything but the chia seeds in a Nutri Bullet. *This is important.*
3. Pulse the ingredients for only a few seconds. Then remove the bullet stand and mix with a rubber spatula.
4. Place back on the blender and pulse again for a few seconds. (We do not want this mixture to be too liquid, caused by over-blending.) Pulse only a few more seconds or until a batter has formed.
5. Remove from the blender stand and fold in the chia seeds.
6. Add 1 cup of batter to the waffle iron and cook.

Makes two! YUM!

Breakfast Bread Pudding: Berry

We live in a fast-paced world. Americans are constantly looking for quick, convenient ways to make delicious dishes. These bread puddings are both excellent recipes to begin the morning right or for yummy afternoon desserts. I love them because they are fresh, homemade, and delicious.

ATTENTION: Side Bar!!

There ARE sugar and fat in these recipes (although the natural kind!)

I would recommend having this treat maybe once a week and not every day!

Again, Mess and I would like to stress *balance* in our book. Many of our athletes are kids, and they like to have fun and enjoy sweets. Many of these recipes *do* have a lot of healthy calories, some more than others. Be smart and practice balance. We would rather you eat healthy calories in abundance rather than processed snack cakes, sodium-laden cupcakes, and candy bars or cereal like Lucky Charms or Fruit Loops. Real, whole foods are preferable for snacking rather than synthetic bars and drinks! Now...

Back to our bread :)

Mug and "cup" breads, muffins, and puddings have become popular all over the world recently, but in France, they have used this technique for a while. Americans are catching on! Read the directions closely, as they are important to gaining the right texture.

Tools

> ✶   You need microwave-safe mugs for these recipes, (We have our favorites in our store, www.betsymcnally.com)

Serves One to Two

Nutrition:

Calories per Serving: 500
Sodium: 486mg
Sugar: 42g
Carbohydrate: 69g
Protein: 12.1 g

Prep Time: 10 minutes

Cook Time: 3 minutes

Ingredients:

3/4 cup blueberries, raspberries, and strawberries

1 tablespoon melted, real, whole butter

1 teaspoon raw turbinado sugar

3 tablespoons almond milk

1 tablespoon flour

1 egg

Steps:

1. In a pot on the stove, cook the red fruits, sugar, and butter over medium heat. Simmer for five additional minutes.
2. Into a microwave-safe mug, add the fruit mixture, followed by the 3 tablespoons of almond milk. Stir with a fork.
3. Next, add the egg (NOTE: always add the egg *after* the almond milk so it doesn't cook) Mix with the fork well until thoroughly blended.
4. Add the tablespoon of flour and continue to stir well.
5. Place in the microwave for one minute. It depends on how strong your microwave is in terms of thorough cooking.

BE CAREFUL: the *mug* and *ingredients* are Extremely Hot! Wait a few minutes before eating, and check the temperature before doing so. (The food continues to cook after it has left the microwave so attention) Enjoy!

Breakfast Bread Pudding: Chocolate

This one is more for a "quick dessert." Dark chocolate is a known antioxidant, great for your health, and helps to release serotonin. (Read more on this in my Superfoods section at the end of the book!)

Serves One or Two to Share!

Prep Time: 5 minutes

Cook time: 2 minutes

Nutrition:

> Calories Per Serving: 600
> Sodium: 565mg
> Sugar: 45g
> Carbohydrate: 60g
> Protein: 13.5 g

Ingredients:

> **1/4 cup** dark chocolate chips, 65 % cocoa
>
> **1 tablespoon** of melted butter
>
> **1 egg**
>
> **3 tablespoons** almond milk
>
> **1/2 teaspoon** vanilla extract
>
> **1 teaspoon** raw brown sugar
>
> **1 tablespoon** flour

Steps:

1. Melt the chocolate and butter in the microwave-safe mug for 30 seconds.
2. Remove from microwave. Stir the butter and chocolate well with a fork, so you don't have an explosion in the microwave later! If the butter isn't melted, cook for another 30 seconds. Be sure *not* to overcook.
3. Add the almond milk and continue to stir.
4. Add the sugar and vanilla. Continue to stir for another 30 seconds.
5. Add the egg. Continue to stir until thoroughly mixed.
6. When there is a nice dark color, add the flour, and keep stirring until smooth.
7. Place in the microwave for 1 minute.

Wait 2 to 3 minutes to eat, because it will be very hot!

Enjoy!

Betsy's Thoughts: Overcoming an Excuse-Making Mindset

I DON'T CLAIM to be perfect in any sense of the word. However, it does bother me when I hear people making excuses about nutrition. Please remember: my job is to coach people in the areas of fitness and nutrition, so I'm going to hold people accountable to these standards, if they ask for my help. There has to be some level of discipline to being healthy, all within a balanced approach.

Yes, I understand it's not always easy to eat clean, organic food.

Yes, I understand it's not always easy to eat the most healthy choices when you're traveling or in situations where healthy food is not available.

I understand that healthy food isn't always available, and sadly for some, it isn't always financially possible for people to eat healthy (which, in fact, is a whole other book I want to write: cheap food is killing us; you have to spend more money to get the good stuff. Something wrong with that...) I have had people contact me about creating meal plans for athletes on foods stamps, too. This is an area I would truly love to explore more, in the future. I know it is a huge issue on this country.

However, I believe people who have the opportunities and means to do so should make every attempt possible to put their nutrition and their health as priorities. I applaud those who do so. I know they are out there!

It's no secret that, in America, we have huge issues with obesity, hypertension, heart disease, and other debilitating and even life-threatening sicknesses.

Again, I realize there are a lot of socioeconomic issues tied into this debate, but for the sake of this thought, I want to keep this focused on education. I want to help people at least *try* to eat the best options possible (e.g., choosing a 99-cent apple over a 99-cent bag of potato chips...)

I believe there comes a time for everyone to stop making excuses and to make nutrition a priority. In my experience, the issue comes down to priority and preparation. A little preparation can go a long way: extend life, fend off sickness, and help people to get off medications and live healthier lives.

My question is, what good are we, if we don't have our health? If we are *not* healthy, fit, and feeling good about ourselves, then what good is a vacation to Disney World? A ride in a fancy car? A trip around the world?

What good is a beautiful swimming pool in our backyard, if we don't want to get in a bathing suit?

What is the good in attending a party or an event or traveling the world, if our hearts aren't functioning properly or we are so out of shape that we have to rent scooters to get around an amusement park?

What good is spending thousands of dollars in the sport of gymnastics, if we are fueling our athletes on processed, nutrient-poor, lifeless foods?? How can we expect to run like amazing machines for four hours when we're eating chips and soda?

This isn't just about the children or athletes. It's about the adults in charge, too. And what if we aren't healthy enough to enjoy our kids' weddings and attend sporting events or we don't have enough energy to play with our toddlers and grandchildren?

Oftentimes, I see people in grocery stores carting themselves around in scooters simply because they are overweight. If someone is legitimately injured or in need of a wheelchair, of course. I get it. However, for people who are overweight and out of shape, they really should be using that time to walk around and burn some calories. Human beings are made to move. We are hunters and grazers. We're made to walk around. We are made to run.

To break it down into simple terms, I always tell my athletes ask yourself this question:

What did a cave woman eat?

She ate nuts, fruits, berries, seeds, fish, plants, wild game/animals, and roots. (Many of the things you will find in this book.)

She didn't eat macaroni and cheese!

If you are struggling with making nutrition a priority, please don't think I'm yelling at you. In fact, I am cheering for you. I want you to *live*.

Start slow and start simple but start changing.

This weekend, I held my Betsy Bootcamp at Tupelo Gymnastics Center in Tupelo, Mississippi. It was the fifth time I'd brought my camp to the gym. Just one year before, I gave a traditional educational seminar on clean eating.

This year, a man by the name of Tommy stood up. I remembered him from the year before, but I wasn't sure if it was him, because I didn't even recognize him.

He told me I had changed his life with my clean-eating seminar. He had lost 100 pounds since I last saw him a year before.

I was completely floored, and it brought me to tears.

Just by making some simple changes in lifestyle: cutting out fast food, processed food, and soda, and eating more functional, fresh fruits and vegetables, his family had completely changed their lifestyle. Even his eleven-year-old daughter, a gymnast at the gym, came back looking healthier and stronger. I didn't recognize her, either!

Now, I am not an advocate for children losing weight. But when a child (whether they play sport or not) is severely obese, overweight, or even underweight, there is definitely a need for a lifestyle change. This family completely defines the point of this message. I am so incredibly proud of them for taking their lives into their own hands. They are amazing.

The lesson?

If you are making excuses, stop. Or live with the consequences. The consequences could be lack of performance in your sport, lack of health, and creating unhealthy habits for a lifetime.

This family is living proof that lifestyle change *is* possible.

As I hugged Tommy this past weekend, he told me to wait until next year, because he wasn't finished yet.

I can't wait.

ଓଃଓଃଓଃଓଃ

"Si Dieu devait apparaître aux affamés, il n'oserait leur apparaître que sous forme de nourriture"

(If God were to appear to the hungry, He would dare to appear to them only in the form of food.)

—*Gandhi*

Mess's Thoughts

We eat with our eyes, not our hearts...

ENERGIZING MID-MORNING SNACKS

The Spinach Shake Your Kids Will Love

One of the biggest complaints I get from the parents of my athletes: "My kid won't eat green vegetables!" We try several times throughout the book to hide fruits and veggies in our treats... *Shhhhhhhh...*

This is unfortunately true for a lot of kids who haven't developed their "palate" in terms of green veggies. I always tell my kids, if it's GREEN, it's GOOD (except for a green Gatorade)

Spinach, for example, is an essential food for young, growing athletes because of its powerful folic acid and calcium density, as well as its fiber-rich and anti-inflammatory properties.

Please note: your protein powder will make a difference with this one! If you are using protein powder with artificial sweeteners, there can sometimes be an aftertaste.

I like several different protein powders. However, I feel that there are a number of decent brands on the market. It is a personal and economic choice.

My recommendation is a protein powder that has roughly 30-32 grams of protein per scoop, 120-140 calories, 3-4 grams of healthy fat, 18-22 grams of protein, and 3-4 grams of carbohydrate. Try to keep sugars under 2 grams per serving, and limit artificial sweetening. Sucralose is not recommended, but again this is a personal choice.

I use Plant Fusion's Complete Protein Vanilla in this recipe, which contains a natural-leaf non-chemical sweetener called stevia. If you use this protein, you can omit the honey.

I am not a *huge* fan of most sweeteners, but if you have a kid who absolutely must have a sweeter taste, stevia would be my choice. I actually prefer honey over any other sweetener. For this recipe, you can add in or take out the honey depending on your protein selection.

Tools

* A blender or a Nutri Bullet, available in our store, www.betsymcnally.com.

Makes Two Servings

Nutrition

Calories Per Serving: 206
Fat: 9g
Sodium: 290 mg
Carbohydrates: 22.1g
Sugars: 10.8g
Protein: 20.4 g

Ingredients:

2 cups spinach

1/2 banana

1 tablespoon dark cocoa or black cocoa powder

1 teaspoon honey

1 scoop whey or vegetable protein (**32 grams**)

1 tablespoon natural peanut butter or almond butter

1-1/4 cup almond milk

1 cup ice

Steps:

1. Place all ingredients in the blender.
2. Blend until smooth! Yummy!

Plantain with Coconut and Cocoa

Plantains are a great snack for gymnasts because of their energy-boosting and vitamin-dense richness! They are also a great source of fiber, vitamins A, C, and B-6, and the minerals magnesium and potassium. Plantains are very fibrous, much like a potato, and they are also loaded with antioxidants, which are great for immunity building. The B-6 is very useful for giving our athletes lots of energy!

This recipe is inspired by a work experience that Mess had here in the States. He was working in a kitchen at a college that made fried plantains and they "killed the recipe," in his own words. Their recipe deep-fried and overcooked the plantains, going through multiple processes like double frying and then baking. Most of the nutritional value of the plantain was lost by the end of the process. He wanted to make the cleanest version of this recipe that kept the vitamins and nutrients intact.

Serves Two (to make more, just add the same amount of ingredients to make another)

Nutrition

Calories Per Serving: 253
Sodium: 4mg
Fat: 9.8g
Sugar: 22.1g
Carbohydrate: 40g

Ingredients:

1 **large** plantain

1 **tablespoon** coconut Oil

1 **tablespoon** honey

1 **teaspoon** cinnamon

1 **teaspoon** black cocoa powder

Steps:

1. Since the skin of the plantain is very tough, it's best to open the plantain like this: with a sharp knife, make 3 long slices down the sides of the plantain. Then slowly, delicately peel back the skin.
2. Slice the plantain in two pieces lengthwise.
3. In a sauce pan, add 1 tablespoon of coconut oil to medium heat. It will melt quickly. Then place the plantain on its backside into the pan.
4. Cook the plantain for five minutes, then flip the banana for another 5 minutes on the other side.
5. Place the banana on a plate and add the tablespoon of honey, cinnamon, and cocoa powder.
6. Wait 2 minutes so the plantain becomes softer before eating.
7. If you want an even softer plantain, place it in foil and close, wait 10 minutes, and serve!

Delicious, non-processed and chock full of vitamins, minerals, and energy!

M' Energy Bar

(Mess's Energy Bar!)

This is a delicious pre-workout pump-up energy bar. One of my biggest issues as a sports nutritionist is the extraordinarily large number of protein snacks, bars, and energy bars loaded with sugar alcohols, sodium, and excessive additives that line our grocery store shelves. A lot of the time, many of these bars are nothing more than glorified candy bars with an excessive amount of sugar, preservatives, fillers, and added vitamins and minerals that can lead to constipation, diarrhea, gas, and bloating. The M'energy (Mess's Energy Bar) is pure, simple, and delicious. Make a batch, and pop them in lunch bags for a quick grab-and-go snack!

I know you will love these, because Mess has made several batches and brought them to Cincinnati Gymnastics to give them to my training athletes post-workout. Several times, they have asked me for this recipe. Well, girls, here it is!

Makes 15 servings

Tools

* ✱ A 9-inch baking dish

Nutrition

Calories Per Serving: 132
Sodium: 1 mg
Fat 4mg
Sugar 6.7 g
Carbohydrate: 22.2 g
Protein: 3.7 g

Ingredients:

2 ripe bananas

3-1/2 cups dry, rolled oatmeal

1/2 cup sliced almonds

1/2 cup dark chocolate chips

2 tablespoons of honey

Steps:

1. Preheat the oven to 355 degrees.
2. Heat a pot on medium heat.
3. Slice banana into small chunks and place in the pot.
4. Add in the honey. For 5 minutes, slowly mix the banana and honey over the heat, so it doesn't burn, mixing and blending as well as you can. It may be a little chunky.
5. In a separate mixing bowl, add the oats, almonds, and dark chocolate chips. Mix those well.
6. Remove the banana mixture from the heat and add it to the bowl with the dry mix. Mix until well blended and you have a fairly smooth consistency.
7. Spread the mix into the baking dish and pack it firmly, so it is even and straight, about an inch thick.
8. Bake in the oven for 20 minutes.
9. Cool for 30 minutes then cut into your favorite size and shape bars.

Enjoy!

Date Cubes

Make a date with our Date Cubes. They are loaded with vitamins, minerals, fiber, and natural sugars to help energize your athletes. These date bars are a great mid-workout fuel-up, as they are a tasty source of simple, natural sugar that will push an athlete during an exhausting practice. The potassium-rich bananas and heart-healthy hazelnuts are any athlete's friend for excellent nerve and muscle function and brain-happy healthy fats!

Mess grew up eating dates. Again, they are a staple snack in North African cuisine and one of the functional foods we connected on, as I have always used them as an energy booster for mid-workout fueling.

These cubes are recommended before workouts or during workouts, if you are feeling tired. You can cover these and keep them in the refrigerator for up to 7 days.

Serves 16/makes 16 cubes

Tools:

- ✳ Kitchen Aid electric mixer with Flex Fan appliance
- ✳ A mold for your date bars. We used Freshware Silicone Molds for cupcake, muffin, loaf, protein and energy bars. (In our store.)

Nutrition:

Calories per 2 cubes: 65   Sodium: 0 mg
Fat: 1.5g   Calories: 65
Sugar: 8.5g   Carbohydrate: 13g
Protein 2g

Ingredients:

7 ounces pitted dates

1 teaspoon 100% raw cacao powder

3 tablespoons coconut flour

2 tablespoon crushed hazelnuts

1/2 large ripe banana

Steps:

1. Place all ingredients in your Kitchen Aide Mixing Bowl.
2. Slowly mix all ingredients with the Kitchen Aide Flex Fan attachment.
3. If you don't have an electric mixer, finely chop the dates into very tiny small pieces and mix all the ingredients by hand.
4. After mixing until smooth, form into a ball.
5. Prepare your mold. Take small pieces of the mixture and stuff into the squares of the mold. It is okay if you don't fill every mold—you will probably only fill 4 of them—but pack each square to the top.
6. Place the mold, uncovered, into the refrigerator.
7. Leave the bars in the refrigerator for a minimum of 3 hours, however the longer the better, for these bars to be the perfect consistency. (4 hours recommended)
8. Remove the mold and carefully remove each date bar.
9. Slice each bar into 4 even cubes.
10. Enjoy!

Betsy's No Bake Protein Bars

This recipe is an athlete favorite because it is hearty and light at the same time, and it's also very delicious. It is all natural and void of preservatives, sodium, added sugar, and other fillers that you will find in many protein bars on the market. Great for a pre-workout or mid-workout fuel-up, it boasts heart-healthy oatmeal, energy-boosting chia seeds, and protein-packed almond butter. Lots of fiber, healthy fat, and deliciousness every gymnast will love!

Also, chia seeds will expand in your stomach, giving the feeling of fullness. That is why I also recommend this bar for breakfast, as it will keep you satisfied throughout the morning hours.

By the way, choose a protein you like, but watch for fillers and extra sodium and sugar. We used Plant Fusion Complete Protein Creamy Vanilla Bean. It does contain stevia, but there are many other proteins on the market that are sweetener-free. This is a personal choice, so do what is best for you!

Makes about 8-10 protein bars, depending on your mold

Tools:

* A mold (We use Freshware Silicone Mold, for Cupcake, Muffin, Loaf, Protein Bars, 9-Cavity—in our store, www.betsymcnally.com)
* Protein powder (We use Plant Fusion Complete Protein Creamy Vanilla Bean, which you can find in our store)

Nutrition:

Calories Per Serving: 275

Sodium: 20mg

Fat: 17g

Sugar: 11g

Carbohydrates: 25

Protein: 12

Ingredients

1 cup almond flour

1 cup rolled oats

1/2 cup protein powder

1/4 cup chia seeds

1/4 cup coconut flakes

1/4 cup raisins

1 cup coconut milk

1 cup almond butter

1/4 cup raw honey

Steps:

1. In a large mixing bowl, add almond flour, oats, protein powder, chia seeds, raisins, and coconut flakes. Mix well with a rubber spatula.
2. In a separate bowl, mix together the coconut milk, almond butter, and honey. Mix well with a rubber spatula.
3. Add the wet mixture to the dry mixture and stir well until completely blended together.
4. Grab your mold. Press mixture evenly into the mold squares.
5. Place the mold in the refrigerator uncovered for 4-6 hours or until firm.

Artichoke Guacamole

This recipe is delicious and quick, great for a party of gymnasts or other athletes who want to get the amazing benefits from artichokes and enjoy a delicious snack, too. (I also brag a lot about artichokes in the Gratin of Artichokes with Salmon and Boursin recipe, but here is more!)

Artichokes are an amazing vegetable. They are loaded with vitamins, minerals, even protein, and tons of fiber. Artichokes are a food that Mess grew up with. There are so many different ways to eat them: in soups, purées, dips, boiled, or baked. I always say I could write a cookbook with just sweet potatoes, and Mess says the same thing about artichokes!

Tools:

* A bullet or blender for this recipe (available in our store www.betsymcnally.com)

Serves 4

Nutrition

Calories Per Serving: 106

Sodium 1900 BEFORE rinsing. (When you rinse, you cut this dramatically, almost) in half

Fat: 1g

Carbohydrate: 20g

Sugar: 4.5g

Protein: 5.5 g

Ingredients:

2 12-ounce jars artichoke hearts (we use Delallo marinated artichoke hearts)

1 small tomato

1 small shallot

1 teaspoon fresh coriander

1 teaspoon lemon juice

1/4 teaspoon cayenne pepper

1/2 teaspoon salt

1/2 teaspoon pepper

Steps:

1. Drain the artichokes and rinse well with cold water to remove the vinegar.
2. Then boil the artichokes for 10 minutes with a little salt. This will make the artichokes softer and take away a lot of the vinegar taste.
3. Let them dry for a few minutes.
4. Place them in a bullet or blender.
5. Cut the tomato and place pieces in the bullet, along with the shallot and all other ingredients.
6. Blend for 30 seconds.
7. Eat with organic tortilla chips!

Lentil Hummus (With Carrots, Celery, Cucumbers, and Pita)

We wanted to create a "different" version of classic hummus with something that is delicious and nutritious but also a twist on traditional chick pea recipes.

Growing up, I didn't eat lentils much, but Mess did. His mother was constantly cooking them and touting them for their health benefits. She frequently made a lentil stew. He remembers her making the stew especially during the winter months, to keep the family healthy. He remembers her describing the vitamins, minerals, and immunity-boosting properties.

In addition, Mess is a huge fan of hummus and Lebanese food. We wanted to do something with lentils, so he came up with this delicious take on traditional hummus. It is packed with fiber, protein, zinc, and magnesium, which are all healthy vitamins and minerals for strong bones and immunity.

Servings 4-6

Tools:
* A Nutri Bullet (in our store, www.betsymcnally.com)
* Rubber Spatula

Prep Time: 20 minutes + soak your lentils for 24 hours in water

Nutrition:

Calories Per Serving: 198   Sodium 575mg

Fat: 12.5g   Carbohydrate 19

Sugar: 2.5   Protein 7g

Ingredients

8 ounces of soaked lentils (soak in water for 24 hours; use enough water to cover the beans completely *plus* an extra 3 cups)

1/2 cup water from beans that have been soaked

1 tablespoon olive oil

2 tablespoons lemon juice

1 teaspoon salt

1 tablespoon tahini

1.5 tablespoon minced garlic

Paprika for topping

Carrots, celery and cucumbers or pita bread for dipping

Steps:

1. In a bullet, blend the soaked lentils with 1/2 cup of soaking water. Blend until creamy but still thick. You may need to add a little more water, so the blended consistency is smooth.
2. Add 1 tablespoon of olive oil and blend for a few more seconds.
3. Remove the lentil mixture with a rubber spatula and place in a bowl.
4. Add tahini to mixture and blend well with a rubber spatula. Then add in the lemon juice and blend.
5. Add in the salt and garlic, and blend well. Top with paprika, and you are reading for dipping! YUM!

Betsy's Thoughts: My Philosophy on Food Timing For Gymnasts

FOOD TIMING is a big issue that many parents and coaches ask me about for their athletes. I spend a lot of time lecturing and advising on this topic, and the answer is there isn't one right answer....

The issue with food timing is that a lot of gymnasts have strange schedules. Some of them are homeschooled, some of them go to full-time school, and some have evening practices that disrupt the normal eating patterns of the day. Oftentimes, parents will ask me if it is okay for their kid to eat at 10 p.m., after practice. (The short answer: yes). A lot of times, gymnasts are eating in the car, and their parents struggle, wondering if giving them fast food on the way home is the best option. (The short answer: no!)

When devising a nutritional program for gymnasts, each athlete is completely different. What I give an elite athlete who is home-schooled and training six hours a day will look completely different from that of an Xcel athlete training eight hours a week and going to regular school.

In addition, we consider the level of commitment of the parents to pack dinners and snacks for travel.

Every situation is completely different. Many kids have food allergies, aversions, strong texture issues, dislikes of certain foods, or can't digest certain foods. This will impact food choices.

I always tell my athletes and parents to get ready to be *uncomfortable* when and if starting a new food regime or plan. Being open to change is so very crucial to success. For some it's not easy, although it may in fact be just

what the athlete needs to take it to the next level. Oftentimes, during the first few weeks of a program, there is a lot of resistance if a kid isn't ready to eat every two to three hours, which is challenging for some who are used to only eating three times a day.

I feel it's very important to know, understand, and connect with each individual athlete. If you are having an issue trying to create a program for your kid, it's really important first to start with education on clean eating and how processed foods affect the athlete. To let them know it's imperative to fuel properly for the sport. To help them see the connection between what they put in their body and how they feel or perform. Most of these kids are training 16-24 hours a week. How many kids do you know, other than gymnasts, who train 16-24 hours a week? Some professional athletes don't even train that much. This sport takes special fueling.

In addition, the athlete must be informed about the importance of hydration. Gymnasts should consistently be hydrating throughout the day—before practice, during, and after, as well.

Sometimes, gymnasts will deprive themselves of water because they feel it will make them feel bloated or heavy. However, this is completely untrue. Water in equals water out! The body will actually hold onto water if you deprive it of hydration. It's also important to eat nutrient-dense foods like spinach, asparagus, broccoli, and lots of green vegetables and vitamin-rich fruits, to help with hydrating the body properly.

I've noticed that oftentimes gymnasts think they're tired because they're not eating enough food, when it's not food they're lacking but water and hydrating foods.

Gymnasts should try to drink close to their full body weight in ounces every single day. I recommend the athlete get a water app on their phone, to remind them it's time to drink!

Back to timing. I will cover this topic specifically in part two of the book (Betsy's Gymnastics Kitchen), but I want to preface those articles by saying, *Everyone Is Different,* so please be open to trying out what works for you.

One thing is for certain: all gymnasts need to eat every 2.5 to 3.5 hours, no questions asked.

That means snacking before, during, and after practice, if necessary. Again, some kids cannot handle food in their stomach right before practicing gymnastics, and that's totally understandable. But some kids can, and they need this instant energy. We are all different. That's why I create individual meal recommendations for this reason alone. (Keep in mind when comparing an Xcel gymnast to an Elite gymnast, this is going to look different.)

All gymnasts should try to eat small meals frequently throughout the day. Other sports like long-distance running, swimming, football, basketball, or ice hockey will require different fueling and are more cardiovascular-based. If ever in doubt, go by the 2.5 to 3.5-hour rule: if you haven't eaten within that time range, grab a snack!

"Pas d'artifice en cuisine pour déguiser une nourriture sans goût"

(Don't add artificial products to disguise the real taste)

—Spanish Proverb

ଙ୍ଙ୍ଙ୍ଙ

Mess's Thoughts:

If you trust in your products and use fresh foods, you won't need to disguise with artificial colors, flavors, and fillers.

NUTRIENT-RICH LUNCHES

Toad Tuna Patties

I created this recipe because tuna is such a great protein source. In addition, tuna is heart-healthy and contains brain-boosting omega-3s. Oh, and why the "*Toad*?" That is actually my nickname, which I earned in college when I was sitting under a blanket in the student lounge. A kid came by and said, "Hey, you look like a *toad* sitting under that blanket!" LOL! Also, my car got "towed" that night, so everyone liked the play on words!

A lot of kids don't love the taste of tuna alone, so I created these delicious patties. The tuna taste is truly hidden, and the patties don't have much of a "fishy" taste. The oatmeal for energy, the broccoli for fiber, and the eggs for vitamin B-12 energy boosting are a great way to load up on nutrients, post-workout. Don't forget about the lutein-rich tomatoes found in salsa—great for those gymnast's eyes!

Makes 3 Patties

Nutrition

Calories Per Serving (1 Patty): 123
Protein: 10
Sodium: 747mg
Fat: 6.9 g
Sugar: 1g
Carbohydrates: 6.1 g

Ingredients

1 2.6-ounce can/pack low-sodium white albacore tuna

3 tablespoons oats

1 egg

1 egg white

1 teaspoon sea salt

1 teaspoon cumin

1 teaspoon onion powder

1/4 cup finely diced raw broccoli (the crowns)

2 tablespoons salsa

1 tablespoon coconut oil

Steps:

1. In a bowl, chop tuna into fine little pieces with a fork.
2. Add the sea salt, cumin, and onion powder. Continue to chop.
3. Then add in the egg, egg white, and oats. Mix thoroughly with the fork and then a spatula.
4. Add in the diced broccoli pieces. Mix all together until a thick batter is formed.
5. Place 1 tablespoon coconut oil in a pan. Heat over medium-high heat.
6. Pour out the batter in three patties or pancakes. Cook until brown on the other side and flip.
7. Push down on the patties with a spatula and let cook until brown in the other side.
8. Serve with a tablespoon of salsa per patty. YUMMY lunch date with the TOAD!

Green Soup

Greens are an essential for any athlete's nutrition program. Why?

They provide numerous vitamins, minerals, and antioxidants. They help with inflammation, build immunity, boost energy, and are water-dense. A lot of times, kids don't want to *eat* greens, but this soup is so tasty, they won't be able to object to eating them! You can also make this batch, freeze it, and pull it out on cold winter days. This is one of my favorite recipes, one that Mess's mother taught him.

I first learned about making soup from Mess when I visited him in France. We had a whole bunch of green veggies left over, and one morning I found him boiling them and putting them in a blender. "What in the *heck* are you doing?" I wondered.

He was making soup, and boy did I love it. So will you.

Servings (1 cup): 16 = enough for an army!

Tools:

* A Kitchen Aide hand blender (available in our store, www.betsymcnally.com)

Nutrients:
Calories: 150 per serving
Sodium: 133mg
Fat: 7.4g
Calories: 150
Sugar: 4.9g
Carbohydrates: 19.8g
Protein: 4.5 g

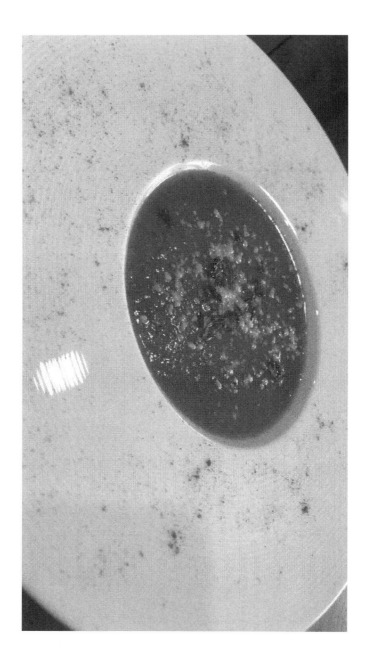

Ingredients:

3 **tablespoons** olive oil

1 **clove** garlic, diced

1/2 white onion, diced fine

1/2 small turnip, scraped and sliced

1 yellow squash, sliced and diced

1 head broccoli

1 small potato, washed

2 **cups** spinach

4 large celery sticks

2 leeks, remove the end and top; just use the white root

1 bunch of collard greens (about 2 **cups**)

1/4 **cup** fresh organic tomato sauce

Dash of paprika

1 **tablespoon** parsley

1 **teaspoon** powdered/grated parmesan

Steps:

1. Place everything but the collard greens and spinach in a large pot filled with water just to the height of the veggies.
2. Add 1-3 teaspoons of salt, and let sit on high heat until boiling.
3. Reduce heat to medium and cover. Keep at a very low boil for 15 minutes.
4. Then add the green spinach and collards. Cover again and, at low heat, let boil for another 45 minutes.
5. Remove from heat and let sit for 30 minutes.
6. With an electric hand mixer, carefully blend the ingredients until smooth. Add salt and pepper to taste. Be careful when using the mixer, and be sure to use a large enough pot.
7. Top with fresh parsley, paprika, and parmesan. Enjoy this soup in the winter! Bon Appetit!

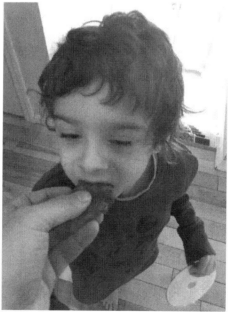

Lenny eating a sardine patty

Lenny's Sardine Patties

I love sardines for gymnasts for many reasons, but the main one is the amazing amount of omega fatty acids they have, for brain health.

Everyone knows that gymnastics is a very technical sport. The more brain foods we can get into our athletes' bodies, the better! I also love how they have both calcium and vitamin D, for bone health, and the large amount of protein in each serving of sardines. Your kids may pinch their noses, but even Lenny, our autistic child with food aversions, loves this recipe! Hence the name~!

In addition, Mess's mother made sardines all the time in France, so it is something he grew up eating. Must be in the blood, because Lenny fell in love with them, too. I didn't know this before, but I guess fresh sardines are extremely abundant and an important part of the North African diet, especially in those regions close to the sea. Sardines are also popular in the south of France, especially in coastal areas. Mess lived for some time in Marseilles, and he does confirm this delicacy is very popular and enjoyed often in the beautiful south of France.

Tools

* Your hands (gloved, if you want to) or a Kitchen Aid electric mixer (available in our store, www.betsymcnally.com) with the **flat flex edge attachment ONLY**.
* A frying pan.

Makes Three Servings

Nutrition

Calories Per Serving: 271

Sodium: 586mg

Fat: 21.9g

Sugar: 0.8g

Carbohydrates: 1.6g

Protein: 18.1 g

Ingredients:

2 3.75-ounce tins sardines with no bones, soaked in olive oil (there will be three fish inside)

1 egg

1/2 teaspoon onion powder

1/2 teaspoon garlic powder

NO SALT!

Black pepper to taste

A pinch of cayenne pepper

1 tablespoon chopped parsley

1 tablespoon powdered parmesan cheese

2 tablespoon fresh tomato sauce

3 tablespoons coconut oil

Lemon juice to taste, fresh tomato slices, or salsa

Instructions

1. Drain the oil from the sardines well.
2. Place the sardines in a bowl first.
3. Then add *all* the other ingredients to the bowl *except* the coconut oil and lemon juice. (The oil is for the pan to cook the patties.)

4. Thoroughly mix everything in the bowl, mashing and mixing all ingredients together. The sardines will break apart and are very fragile. Do this for three minutes. (If using the electric mixer, mix for three minutes as well.)

5. Divide the mix into small balls about the size of ping-pong balls. Place them on a plate.

6. Add the coconut oil to your pan and heat over medium heat.

7. When warm, gently place the balls in the pan. Let them cook three minutes and then delicately, slowly flip each ball without breaking it. When it flips over, press down with the fork, and push into a patty.

8. Cook for three more minutes. If you would like the patty more crusty, you can cook longer.

9. Remove your patties with a spatula and or fork.

PLEASE NOTE: DO NOT EVER ADD SALT TO THIS RECIPE! You can eat this with an arugula, endive, or green salad and a squeeze of lemon juice or fresh tomatoes or salsa.

E-Z Ezekiel European-Style Pizza

Who doesn't love pizza? European pizza is completely different than American pizza, as I learned when I moved to France! While living in Europe, I learned that pizza is fresh and actually healthy and good for you. This particular pizza is loaded with heart-healthy fat, calcium-rich cheese, vitamin-dense arugula, and protein-packed salmon. You can also use chicken, turkey, or tuna, if you want to replace the smoked salmon, but we encourage you to try the omega richness of the salmon. This recipe is quick, yummy, and you can personalize it, too!

Here's a funny story about Americans and *our* pizza. Recently, Mess was working in a restaurant and decided to make a traditional, healthy European pizza. The clients weren't too happy. They asked, "Where is the fat?? Where is the cheese??"

That is when Mess really started to understand how Americans have changed the whole makeup of pizza. Americans have over-crusted, over-cheesed. and over-oiled our pizzas. This is *not* how traditional pizza is made.

We wanted to make Europe's concept of pizza. Europeans eat salmon, goat cheese, and very fine crust on their pizzas. The pizza is cooked with olive oil and not as much cheese. Another example of how we have overdone, supersized, and gone above the simplicity of pizza. Try this out. we hope you are open to the simplicity of it!

Serves: 2

Prep Time: 10 minutes

Tools

> ✱ A traditional baking sheet or pizza pan

Nutrition:

> Calories: 530 for 1 whole pizza
> Sodium: 1628mg
> Fat: 31.8g
> Sugar: 2g
> Carbohydrates: 26.3g
> Protein: 35 g

Ingredients:

> **1** Ezekiel wrap, extra-large if possible (available in the frozen section of your grocer; if not, use a whole-grain wrap or extra-large tortilla wrap)
>
> **1 tablespoon** fresh organic tomato sauce
>
> **1 tablespoon** powdered/ground parmesan cheese
>
> **1/4 cup** goat cheese
>
> **1 teaspoon** drizzled olive oil
>
> **2 ounces** smoked salmon (if you aren't a salmon fan, you can substitute tuna or 2 ounces pre-cooked chicken or turkey)
>
> **1/4 cup** arugula soaked in an additional **1 teaspoon** olive oil
>
> (optional items: sardines, anchovies, capers, olives)

Steps:

1. Preheat your oven to 400 degrees.
2. On your Ezekiel wrap, spread the tomato sauce evenly, covering the entire wrap.
3. Sprinkle on the parmesan cheese, goat cheese, salmon or other meat, and the drizzle of olive oil.
4. Bake 400 for 10 minutes.
5. Remove from the oven, and add 1/4 cup arugula soaked in a teaspoon of olive oil.

Bon Appetit!

GymnaBurger

This burger is inspired by our traditional fast food, American Burger.

When Mess first moved here from France, he admits, he was obsessed with the American burger. He was fascinated with the drive-thrus *everywhere*. You see, in France they do not have half or even a quarter of the fast-food choices we have. Fast Food Disneyland is what Mess saw when he first moved here, and he paid the price. He gained some unhealthy weight, lost a lot of energy, and felt tired, sore, and sick all the time. When he finally realized that fast food was making him sick, he came to his senses and understood why Americans were struggling with obesity, heart disease, and high blood pressure.

This burger is delicious and healthy. Avoid the drive-thru with this at-home delight! Loaded with protein, vitamin B for energy, antioxidant-full spinach, and some cheese for fun and extra protein! Every gymnast needs energy in a clean way. You don't have to eat fast food to get your fix!

Servings: Makes one burger

Tools:

* A pastry cutter, if you want the perfect egg center (available in our store)

Nutrition:

Calories Per Serving: 500

Fat: 23 g

Sodium: 1160

Carbohydrates: 23g

Sugar: 4.2 g

Protein: 40g

Ingredients

4 ounces ground turkey

1/4 teaspoon salt

Pinch pepper

1 teaspoon olive oil

1/2 teaspoon onion powder

1 teaspoon parsley

1 slice tomato

1 egg

Handful of spinach

1 whole-grain bun

1 slice mozzarella cheese (organic or low sodium)

Steps:

1. In a mixing bowl, mix ground turkey with salt, pepper, olive oil, onion powder, and parsley. Form into a ball.
2. Place in a frying pan over medium heat. Cook five minutes each side or to your liking. After turning, press down to make a patty.
3. At the same time, place the bun in the toaster.
4. In a small bowl, crack your egg, and scramble with a fork.
5. Next, place another frying pan over medium heat. Add the teaspoon of olive oil and the spinach.
6. When the spinach begins to wilt, with your spatula, mix the scrambled egg into the spinach, and make it into a patty. (If you want a perfectly round egg patty, *here* is where you can

use the pastry cutter. Try not to scramble the egg but form it into a patty, if you are not using the pastry cutter.)

7. Once the egg is cooked, place it on a small plate. Add a little salt and pepper.
8. After everything is cooked, place the egg patty on the bread with the turkey patty. Top with cheese and tomato.

Bon Appetit!

Four-Bean Feta and Sesame Salad

This dish is great in the summer as a side dish alongside grilled meats and veggies. Beans and legumes are instrumental in developing strong bones and connective tissues. They include vitamins and minerals, like potassium and magnesium, and of course muscle-building protein.

Beans are also packed with zinc. Zinc not only helps to repair tissues of the body, but it is *imperative* in maintaining and preventing the *immune system* from breaking down!

In addition, apple cider vinegar is a great prebiotic. This means it aids in digestion and allows for better absorption of probiotic-rich foods. It creates a great environment for proper gut function!

If you have a vegetarian athlete, beans are an amazing source of complex carbohydrates. Be careful, though: beans, beans, the musical fruit...

Serves 6—3/4-cup servings

Nutrition:

Calories: 350 per serving
Sodium: 2273 mg
Fat: 14.7g
Sugar: 14.5g
Carbohydrates: 47.7g
Protein: 21 g

Ingredients

15 ounces Great Northern Beans

15 ounces garbanzo beans

15 ounces kidney beans

1 cup defrosted or fresh edamame soy beans

3 tablespoons raw honey

4 tablespoons apple cider vinegar (organic with the "mother")

1 cup fresh feta cheese

1 tablespoon sesame seeds

2 tablespoons fresh parsley chopped

2 tablespoons sesame seed oil

1 teaspoon salt

1 teaspoon pepper

Steps:

1. Place all of the beans in a large mixing bowl.
2. Add the honey, apple cider vinegar, sesame oil, salt, and pepper, and blend well with the beans.
3. Then add the parsley, sesame seeds, and feta cheese. Fold in well.
4. Let sit for one to two hours covered with plastic wrap for the best, well-mixed taste. Letting your salad sit will let the sauce marinate and make it extra-delicious!

Festive Chick Pea and Purple Kale Salad

Capture the taste of summer in a salad that kids will love! This salad is loaded with vitamin C, healthy fat, antioxidants, and protein. You can also substitute the chick peas and use cooked or grilled chicken, shrimp, or fish, if you prefer.

Legumes like chick peas are packed with zinc, manganese, and calcium for bone health. The purple kale is a powerhouse, full of vitamins, minerals, and an antioxidant called anthocyanin, which helps produce the purple color of the kale. Anthocyanin is known to protect from the cell-damaging effects of the environment.

What you will love most about this salad is the delicious and healthy vitamin C-rich lime salad dressing! *YUM.*

By the way, I learned to make salad dressing from Mess! We Americans generally just plop a tablespoon on our salad and hope it makes its way to every piece of salad. I learned this isn't a very useful technique.

Tip: Take time to whisk the dressing well and toss the salad with the dressing for a good 3 minutes to evenly distribute all of the dressing. A little goes a long way when you do this!

Serves 4
Nutrition:
Calories Per Serving: 255
Sodium: 48mg
Fat: 12g
Sugar: 6.5
Carbohydrate: 30g
Protein: 10g

Ingredients:

5 cups fresh-chopped, cleaned, and washed purple kale

1/2 cup mango slices

1/4 cup chopped purple onion

1/2 cup chopped red pepper

1 sliced avocado

1/2 cup chick peas rinsed and drained

1/2 cup fresh sugar snap peas

1/4 cup finely chopped cilantro

5 cups purple kale

Betsy's Dressing:

1/2 teaspoon honey

1 tablespoon balsamic

4 tablespoons olive oil

1 teaspoon Dijon mustard

1 teaspoon lime juice fresh

Steps:

1. Place all the Betsy's Dressing ingredients in a small bowl and whisk together well.
2. Grab a large salad bowl and place the 5 cups of kale as a base.
3. In sections, add the chopped onions, red pepper, chick peas, snap peas, mango, avocado slices, and cilantro. Arrange in a pattern that you like.
4. Pour the dressing over the entire salad. Remember: toss the salad *well* for a good 3 minutes, turning over and over until the salad is coated in the delicious dressing.

   Enjoy!

Mess's Quick Chicken and Mushroom Quiche

We debated how to make this quiche. We could not have a semi-French cookbook without a quiche!

Of course, Mess wanted a thick, crispy French crust, and I had to put some limits on that because of all the heavy butter and flour. So, we compromised. To make this delicious quiche, you will need a pre-made crust. We loved the one we used for Simple Truth's Thin and Crispy Vegan Crust. Unfortunately, we could not find this product on the Amazon store, so you may have to experiment with the best pizza crust for you.

Quiche Lorraine is well-known and a traditional favorite in France. It boasts a lot of cream, eggs, ham, and a thick, fatty crust! We decided to take this recipe to a healthier level by using the pizza crust, olive oil instead of butter, and chicken instead of ham. We also added powerful shiitake mushrooms, known for their anti-cancer and immunity- building compound called lentinan.

By the way, this recipe was so good, we ate it all in one night. (We wouldn't advise doing that—lol.) We recommend making this the night before and eating it either warmed or cold the next day. Quiche is delicious cold, like pizza! You can eat this for up to two days post-cooking.

This recipe is Betsy's favorite in the book!

Tools:

* A traditional 9-inch pie-baking dish
* Sauté pan

Serves 5-6

Nutrition

Calories Per Serving: 385

Sodium: 1300mg

Fat: 26g

Sugar: 2.5g

Carbohydrates: 10.6g

Protein: 18.6g

Ingredients

2 Simple Truth Thin and Crispy Organic Vegan Pizza Crusts. (You need two because they break easily.) Kroger carries this product, but you can use any organic crust of your choice.

1 6-ounce chicken breast, chopped into small cubes

1-1/2 cups shiitake mushrooms, sliced

1 tablespoon olive oil

6 eggs

1+1 teaspoons salt (1 for eggs)

1 teaspoon pepper

3/4 cup organic whipping cream

2 tablespoons parmesan cheese

3 cups fresh spinach

Steps:

1. Preheat your oven to 350 degrees.
2. Push the two pie crusts into the pie dish. Use two because they break. Before you bake, cut off the excess or "overhanging" parts of the crust from the pie dish.
3. Place the chicken on the pan with the tablespoon olive oil over medium heat.
4. Add the salt and pepper to the chicken.
5. Pre-cook (don't cook all the way through) the chicken for a couple of minutes each side.
6. After pre-cooking the chicken, add the spinach to the pan, and sauté for one minute until wilted a little.
7. In a separate mixing bowl, crack six eggs, and add the cream. Whisk (Mess says, "Violently!" lol) for 3 minutes.
8. Add a teaspoon of salt and continue to beat the eggs and cream together.
9. Add in the parmesan and beat well.
10. In the pie dish, add shiitake mushrooms on top of the crust. Then add in the sautéed mix of chicken and spinach.
11. Pour the cream and egg/cheese mixture over the pie crust filled with chicken.
12. Place in the oven and bake for 45 minutes.
13. Remove from heat after baking and let cool.

Also good served cold or reheated.

Quick Veggie Galette

Love fresh veggies but don't have time to slice, dice, steam, stir fry, and prepare them? Worried that your stock of veggies will go bad before you find time to eat them? This quick veggie galette is your friend and can be a solution to all these preparation issues.

Living in France, I learned so much about eating. One of things I loved and had never seen in America were vegetable galettes. These are vegetable "patties" that you can freeze. They are a quick-option side dish when you don't have time to prepare fresh veggies on the fly. I was amazed that no one in America had figured out these amazing side dishes. They were a staple in our home!

The best thing about these galettes are you can make a batch on Sundays, freeze them, and pop them on the stove for a quick, healthy side dish anytime over the next week or even two. We selected carrots, zucchini, bell pepper, and onion, but feel free to experiment with creating your own galettes!

Tools

* A mold. (We used Freshware Silicone Mold, for Cupcake, Muffin, Loaf, Protein Bars, 9-Cavity. Available in our store, www.betsymcnally.com.)
* Sauté pan

Prep time: 30 minutes

Servings: 9-12 galettes, depending on your mold

Nutrition:

Calories Per Serving: 64

Sodium: 603mg

Fat: 4.6g

Calories: 64

Sugar: 1.4g

Carbohydrates: 4.8g

Protein: 2g

Ingredients:

3 ounces shredded carrots (or **1 cup**)

3 ounces yellow onion sliced (or **1/2 cup,** sliced)

2 organic 4-inch zucchinis

1 bell pepper

1 teaspoon salt

1 teaspoon pepper

1 teaspoon parsley

1/2 teaspoon cumin

2 eggs

2 tablespoons olive oil + more to drizzle

Steps:

1. Slice all veggies lengthwise.
2. Place all ingredients except the eggs together in a large mixing bowl, starting with the veggies. Add olive oil, salt, and pepper last.

3. With a rubber spatula, mix the ingredients (stirring; do not beat—we want the veggies to stay intact). Mix very well until coated with wet mix.

4. Place mixture in a sauté pan and cook for 5 minutes over medium-high heat. Then decrease to medium heat and cook 5 more minutes.

5. Put cooked mixture in a bowl and let cool for ten minutes.

6. After 10 minutes, add the egg and mix well.

7. Using tongs, add the veggie mix into the silicone molds. Push them down evenly in each mold with the back of a spoon. You won't fill each one to the top, so make them even, pressing them down.

8. After pushed down with the rubber spatula add a drizzle of olive oil over each to ensure formation.

9. Place the mold on a cookie sheet or pan to support it as it goes into the freezer. Then cover the mold and the cookie sheet together with plastic wrap and place in the freezer.

10. After the freezing process is finished, remove galette from the mold.

11. Place it in a pan over medium heat and cook for five minutes on each side.

An amazing time-saver and side dish!!

Avocado Burger and Sweet Potato Fries

This recipe takes a little practice, but once you make it once, you will be a pro. Again, as you see throughout this book, we are trying to get athletes to eat a lot of omega-3 fatty acids by way of fish.

The burger itself will be made out of salmon and tuna. The top is actually the avocado. Follow the directions closely to make your perfect bottom-and-top avocado bun!

Mess says this recipe was inspired by a chef in France he never met. He took pieces of his idea that used meat and replaced it with fish. By the way, it is very common in common in France to mix shrimp, salmon, and tuna with avocado.

This recipe is super-beneficial in terms of healthy fat, fiber, vitamins, and minerals. The sweet potato fries are equally delicious and pack a serious dose of vitamin A for strong skin (something a gymnast truly needs!). The benefits of avocado range from potassium to fiber and healthy fat: all essential for a happy, well-functioning athlete for their excellent brain/body connection and anti-inflammatory properties.

Special Note on the sweet potato: I believe sweet potato is probably one of the most perfect foods for a gymnast. I write in more depth about this in my Superfood section, but this is just to highlight a few points here regarding this vegetable root. Sweet potatoes cannot be beat for consistent energy! Gymnasts practice long hours and need complex carbohydrates that take a long time to break down. Be sure to get in one to two sweet potatoes per week for maximum energy, especially at lunch time!

Tools:

- ✳ A pastry cutter (in our store, www.betsymcnally.com)
- ✳ Baking dish

Serves 2 people

Nutrition:

Calories Per Serving: 490

Fat: 25.5g

Sodium: 1700mg

Carbohydrate: 52mg

Sugars: 8g

Protein: 38g

Ingredients:

1 sweet potato (organic preferred)

3.3 ounces smoked salmon

3.3 ounces white albacore tuna

1 teaspoon lime juice

1 teaspoon olive oil

1 teaspoon paprika

1 teaspoon coriander

1 teaspoon parsley chopped

Pinch cayenne pepper

1 teaspoon chopped garlic

1/2 teaspoon salt

1/2 teaspoon pepper

2 slices red onion

1 slice tomato

1 slice provolone cheese

1 avocado, firm (not extra-firm, but not soft)

1 leaf lettuce or kale

1 teaspoon sesame seeds

Steps

1. Preheat oven 350 degrees.

2. Wash your sweet potato well then cut it lengthwise in half. Divide each half in half, so you have 4 pieces. Then cut those in half, so you have 8 total pieces.

3. Place pieces in a bowl. Add the garlic, 1 tablespoon olive oil, the salt, pepper, cayenne pepper, paprika, and parsley. Mix well.

4. Place mixture on a baking dish and bake for 30 minutes.

5. Chop the salmon up into very small pieces on a cutting board. With your fork, chop up the tuna very well.

6. Add together the salmon, tuna, 1 teaspoon of olive oil, the lime juice, pepper, and coriander. Mix well with your hand or a spoon.

7. Place fix mixture in the refrigerator.

SPECIAL: MESS TECHNIQUE

8. Take your avocado. Do not peel it. Cut it lengthwise in half and slowly turn the avocado (one side clockwise, the other side counterclockwise) until the avocado separates. The pit/seed will remain in one half of the avocado.

9. Take a knife and hit the pit/seed squarely in the center. With both hands at the same time, turn the avocado and the seed in the opposite directions, and the seed/pit will pop out.

10. Next take a big spoon and slowly remove the skin from the avocado, trying not to break the avocado. Start by working around the border of the fruit and the skin, loosening it up, until you can remove the avocado in one piece.

11. Place half the avocado on its back. Slice a little off the bottom, if it doesn't balance. This is your *burger base*.

12. Remove the fish from the refrigerator.

13. Place the pastry cutter on a cutting board. Push all the fish inside the pastry cutter to make a patty. Do your best to make the patty as close to the size of the avocado as possible. Remove the pastry cutter, leaving behind the patty.
14. Place the lettuce leaf on top of the avocado.
15. Place your patty on top of the lettuce leaf.
16. Place your slice of cheese on top of the avocado, along with the red onion and tomato, stacking them on "the burger."
17. On a cutting board, sprinkle the other half of the avocado with sesame seeds, and place that on top of the burger.
18. When the potatoes are done in the oven, place them around the burger and voila! A creative and very French take on the burger!

Betsy's Thoughts: Tip for Coaches on Discussing Nutrition

COACHES OFTEN ASK me about how to broach the topic of nutrition with their athletes. Don't get me wrong: I know there are a lot of very knowledgeable coaches and parents out there. However, I believe, when discussing nutrition with gymnasts or other athletes, you should most definitely leave that up to a knowledgeable professional.

I also believe that when gymnastics coaches try to talk to their athletes about nutrition, although well-intentioned, they may not know how to handle the topic. Also, the athlete will do one of two things: they will question the coach's motives in discussing the topic, and/or they will perhaps also judge the coach on their own nutritional choices.

The job of the coach is to coach, and that is why I stay in business—ha-ha! Because my job is to educate about nutrition. As an athlete, I struggled but was never given any solid plans, ideas, or tips on how to fuel. It was just, "Lose weight. Don't eat sugar and no fast food." Ironically, when we would travel as a team, the coach would always stop at Wendy's to feed us. Go figure...

As we all know, gymnastics is a very challenging sport that requires a lot of brainpower, fitness power, flexibility, and balance. Nutrition, as I said before, is the fifth event. It is the coach's responsibility to at least present options to this event, but how the coach chooses to do so needs to be done delicately and with a professional.

I would recommend modeling good behavior yourself. Now, don't get me wrong: you don't have to be fitness guru or even a trainer or nutritionist, but you do have to model healthy, good behavior, so your athletes can follow suit. When traveling together, encourage them to buy their foods at grocery stores and packing healthy snacks. Your athletes will respect you, believe you more, and follow in your path.

Again, I feel this is so important for creating a culture of clean eating in your gym. This goes for parents, as well. Afterall, who is buying the food?

Coaches, here are some tips:

1) Provide opportunities for learning experiences together around food. This includes having parties with healthy food options, going food shopping together while traveling, and doing things socially that revolve around healthy choices for nutrition.

2) Provide an outlet to consistent education, whether through literature, webinars, books, good modeling. This is the only way to create a culture of clean eating. That's where I come in and why a lot of people hire me!

3)Don't be afraid to take the fifth event very seriously. It will help with energy, attitude, and injury prevention, if you find the right fifth event coach! I've seen a huge change and difference in my athletes and coaches who take it seriously.

"Petit á petit, l'oiseau fait son nid."

(Little by little, the bird makes his nest.)

—French Proverb

ଔଔଔଔଔ

Mess's Thoughts:

Changing your eating lifestyle takes time. Don't rush it. Little by little, you can change.

DELICIOUS FUNCTIONAL DINNERS

Coconut Chicken Cordon Bleu and a Side Salad

Mess and I had to work hard to make this classic recipe "Betsy approved" in terms of nutritional value and content. Luckily, we played around with some of the ingredients and made a healthy and delicious meal comparable to a standard Cordon Bleu. We used whole wheat bread instead of white (I wanted whole grain, but I had to compromise), organic chicken, coconut milk instead of heavy cream, and turkey slices instead of ham. Of course, I don't love processed meats, but in life we must have balance and fun—that is one of the biggest messages I want for my athletes. Eat as well as you can and as clean as you can, but we can't all be perfect, and to be perfect isn't healthy either.

Our book wouldn't be complete without a version of Cordon Bleu! This is Mess's favorite meal when he wants to impress clients. Cordon Bleu is normally filled with rich cream sauce, ham, delicious butter, and bread crumbs. He wanted a version that did the recipe justice but was also a cleaner, healthier take. We use coconut oil to cook, for example. Just to note: coconut oil is an MCT oil and has been shown to increase metabolic activity, plus help fend of fungus, as it is anti-fungal and antibacterial. I have my athletes use coconut oil on their skin (the biggest organ of their body), in their hair, and did you know you can even brush your teeth with coconut oil?

Do your best with this recipe. It is absolutely delicious. I recommend cooking it for a special event, a birthday, a holiday, or weekend family dinner! It's absolutely decadent!

Tools:

 ✷ A Nutri Bullet or blender (you can find in our store, www.betsymcnally.com)

Timing Note: We recommend making the bread crumb mixture the day before

Makes 4 servings (2 large chicken breasts cut into four pieces)

Nutrition

Calories per serving: 690

Sodium: 270 mg

Fat: 30g

Sugar: 1.75

Carbohydrates: 18.2g

Protein: 35g

Ingredients

2 6-ounce chicken breasts

1/2 cup rich and creamy (preferred) organic coconut milk canned

4 slices Pepperidge Farm whole wheat bread (what we used; my first choice is a whole-grain bread, but my husband insisted!)

1 teaspoon dry oregano

1 tablespoon onion

1 teaspoon garlic powder

Salt to taste

4 slices organic turkey

4 tablespoons fresh shredded mozzarella cheese

2 tablespoon fresh powdered parmesan cheese

2 eggs

1 cup flour

2 big tablespoons coconut oil

For the salad:

   3 cups arugula

The dressing:

   2 tablespoons olive oil

   1 tablespoon lime juice

   Dash of sea salt and pepper

Steps

1. Whisk together dressing ingredients
2. Preheat your oven to 350
3. Toast the 4 pieces of bread. Wait 10 minutes for the toast to cool.
4. Break the toast apart and place in a Nutri Bullet or blender. Blend bread until powdery.
5. Place bread crumbs on a plate. Add the onion powder, salt, oregano, garlic powder, and salt. Let sit for an hour, but don't cover it or it will become humid. (For the best topping, do this process the day before.)
6. Place washed chicken breast on a cutting board. Imagine an open book. Slice the breast in two, starting from the outside edge, and cut through the middle but do not completely divide it into two separate pieces. You are making an envelope. (If you have a butcher, ask if they will do it for you. Say it's for Cordon Bleu.)
7. Add a pinch of salt and pepper inside breast. Place 2 slices of turkey inside of the chicken "envelope" and 2 tablespoons mozzarella. Slowly close the chicken.
8. Prepare an empty plate and three small mixing bowls.
9. In a small bowl, whisk the two eggs.
10. In another bowl, place the flour.

11. In another bowl, place the bread crumbs mixture.

12. Place both sides of the chicken breast on the flour. Be sure the chicken breast stays closed and both sides are coated. Shake off a bit of the flour.

13. Then dip the chicken in the egg bowl and coat each side. Let the excess egg drip off a bit.

14. Then place it in the bread crumbs mixture, coating both sides well.

15. Place dusted, coated chicken breast on plate.

16. Heat the coconut oil in a frying pan on medium-high heat. After one minute, place the chicken breasts on the pan for 1 minute each side.

17. Then place the chicken on a baking pan and bake it in the oven for 30 minutes.

18. While it's cooking, in a second pot, warm 1 cup of coconut milk on medium heat. Add in salt, pepper, and parmesan cheese. Warning: there may be a little reaction or mini-explosion if the parmesan comes into contact with very high heat.

19. Whisk the milk and cheese for 15 minutes over medium heat. Then set aside but keep it in the pot.

20. Remove chicken from oven. Plate with the cream sauce. Serve with an arugula salad.

Bon Appétit à la coconut!

Pineapple Scallops

Scallops are some of the most protein-dense foods on the planet. In a three-ounce serving, there are twenty grams of protein! Scallops are packed with vitamin B1, excellent for energy and metabolism, and iodine. Iodine is essential for glandular function and helps with mental clarity and memory, as well. Pineapple is one of my favorite fruits for athletes because of its many anti-inflammatory properties and digestive benefits. Put these two superfoods together and you have a meal that even the pickiest gymnast will love.

A lot of our book is influenced by French culture, which is very multicultural in nature. France colonized many island nations, like Martinique, French Polynesia, Guadeloupe, and, at one point, Mauritius Island. Many of these countries adopted the French language and the country of France adopted some of their culinary tastes. This "creole" language and food is widely celebrated all over the world, even in our state of Louisiana, specifically New Orleans and the Bayou.

Mess frequently makes this recipe for his clients. A woman from the Mauritius Islands gave Mess the idea of this pineapple sauce. I, of course, was on board as scallops are loaded with protein and pineapple is one of my favorite vitamin-C-rich fruits that is also great for digestion.

Tools

> ★ A mandolin slicer for the zucchini (we have included one in our store, www.betsymcnally.com)

Serves 2-4

Nutrition:

Calories Per Serving: 403

Sodium: 411mg

Fat: 27.8g

Calories: 403

Sugar: 1g

Carbohydrates: 12.8g

Protein: 30g

Ingredients:

6 large scallops

1/2 a pineapple, cut into cubes (about **one cup**)

2 small organic zucchinis

1 teaspoon chia seeds

1/4 cup microgreens or alfalfa sprouts

1 teaspoon brown sugar

1/2 teaspoon cinnamon

1/2 tablespoon butter

Sea salt and pepper to taste

1/2 teaspoon salt

1/2 teaspoon pepper

1 tablespoon coconut oil

1 tablespoon olive oil

1 tablespoon lime juice

Steps:

1. Remove the center/core of the pineapple and discard. Cut the pineapple into 1 cupful of cubes.
2. Place the pineapple chunks in a pot on medium heat, along with the butter, cinnamon, brown sugar, and pinch of salt. Cook for 10 minutes, stirring.
3. Remove from heat.
4. Heat a tablespoon coconut oil in a nonstick frying pan. Be careful: the coconut oil will get very hot, and a non-stick pan is crucial.
5. Gently add the scallops and cook for five minutes on each side.
6. Slice zucchinis with mandolin slicer or knife.
7. Add zucchini to a sauté pan with a tablespoon of olive oil. Add a pinch of salt and sauté for 5 minutes. Flip and then sauté the other side for five minutes.
8. While the zucchini cooks, put microgreens into a small bowl. Add one tablespoon olive oil, lime juice, and a pinch of salt together. Mix thoroughly.
9. On two plates, place the zucchini in the center of each plate with the scallops on top. Then add the pineapple on the sides.
10. Put sprouts/greens on top of the scallops plus a sprinkle of chia seeds and a dash of pepper.

Bon Appétit!

Parmesan Perch with Brussel Sprouts and Kale

Fish is essential for athletes. I highly recommend two servings per week! Loaded with omega-3 fatty acids, fatty fish is packed with brain-enhancing compounds, helps with inflammation, and is heart-healthy. Please always go for wild fish over farmed fish!

I love this recipe because a lot of times kids are picky about eating fish. This recipe eases them into the taste with a yummy coating that is also good for them. Think of it as fish sticks for athletes! My favorite part of the coating is the minced garlic, which is an anti-fungal powerhouse. Gymnasts are constantly being exposed to fungus in their gyms! Fungus is everywhere, and garlic helps to fend off pesky viruses as well as impair tumor growth. This recipe also includes probiotic-rich Brussels sprouts and vitamin K-abundant kale; an athlete's dream dinner!

Serves 4

Nutrition

> Calories Per Serving: 253
> Sodium: 227
> Fat: 10g
> Carbohydrates: 4g
> Sugar: 1g
> Protein: 36g

Ingredients

1/2 **cup** parsley, finely chopped

1 minced clove of garlic

1/2 **teaspoon** sea salt

1/2 **teaspoon** pepper

2 **tablespoons** olive oil

2 egg whites

1 whole egg

1/2 **cup** shredded parmesan cheese

1 **cup** almond flour

4 6-ounce perch filets

1 **cup** sliced Brussels sprouts

2 **cups** fresh kale

Steps:

1. Preheat oven to 350
2. Prepare a 9-inch baking dish by spreading two tablespoons olive oil evenly on the bottom. Add the fresh minced garlic.
3. In a bowl, crack and scramble the eggs and egg white.
4. In another bowl, mix together the sea salt, pepper, parmesan cheese, almond flour, and parsley.
5. Dip each fish filet into the egg coating then into the flour mixture. Make sure the fish is completely coated with the flour mixture.
6. Place the fish in the baking dish. Line up the filet next to each other.

7. Bake at 350 for thirty minutes or more, fish is cooked through and flakey.

8. While the fish is cooking, clean and halve the Brussels sprouts. Cut the kale into small pieces.

9. Heat another tablespoon of olive oil in a sauté pan. Over medium heat, add the Brussels sprouts and kale, and sauté the veggies for 20-30 minutes or until soft.

10. Add a dash of sea salt and pepper.

11. Remove the fish from the oven and add to a plate with the Brussels sprouts and kale. Bon Appétit!

Seafood Soup

Now, enter Parisian accordion music...

"Les poisson, les poisson, hee-hee-hee, hon-hon-hon!!" (Have you ever seen *The Little Mermaid?)*

I joke with Mess that he is the French chef in the famous Disney movie when he makes this delicious soup.

Don't worry: there are no fish heads in here, but he would love it if there were, because that is the most nutrient-dense part of the fish! I don't think the kids would be happy, though!

Fish soup is a great way to get important omega-3 fatty acids into our athletes to enhance brain function and memory and to help with coaching corrections and confidence. Eating fish two times a week is crucial for cognitive development.

Be ready to have a fishy-smelling kitchen, but it will be worth it! This soup is a great appetizer for a dinner party or lunchtime treat with a salad.

Tools:

* A hand blender in our store, www.betsymcnally.com
* A double-fine mesh strainer, 8 inches (also in the store)

Serves 3-4

Nutrition

Calories Per Serving: 212
Sodium: 1,800mg
Fat: 11g
Sugar: .7g
Carbohydrates: 11g
Protein: 17.1 g

Ingredients

8 ounces wild, large-shelled shrimp, cleaned

3.5 ounces wild perch with skin and bones (yes, it's fine!)

1 small shallot

1 teaspoon lime juice

1 teaspoon salt

Pinch cayenne pepper

Pinch ground pepper

1 300-ml can creamy coconut milk

1/4 cup tomato sauce

2 tablespoons white wine

Parsley for decoration

3 tablespoons olive oil

Steps:

1. Wash and de-shell/de-vein the shrimp. Wash the perch, keeping the skin on the fish, and cut into small cubes.
2. Chop the shallot into small pieces.

3. Heat olive oil in a medium-sized pot over medium heat. Add the shallots and a pinch of salt. Mix with a whisk or rubber spatula.

4. After a minute, add the fish and the shrimp. Increase the heat to medium-high.

5. Once hot, add the white wine and continue to mix. When it begins to boil, lower the heat to medium-low. We call this "déglacer" (deglaze in English), when you add the wine to a warm mixture. A French cooking technique!

6. Next, add the tomato sauce. Mix for one minute on medium heat.

7. Add the can of coconut milk and the pinches of the cayenne and ground pepper.

8. Cover and cook for 10 minutes over medium heat. Check and stir every few minutes.

9. After 10 minutes, remove from the heat.

10. With hand mixer, *carefully* blend the soup at the lowest speed, (we don't want a messy kitchen), until the soup is smooth in texture.

11. When it is smooth, place strainer securely over a mixing bowl or another pot. Pour the soup over the strainer. Using a spoon, mash the pulp so the liquid can easily pass through the strainer. When finished, there should be about two tablespoons of pulp in the strainer. The remaining liquid is your soup!

12. Add the salt and lime juice. Stir well. Top with parsley. Bon Appétit!

Mess's Marinated Chicken Soba (24-Hour Recipe!)

Having family origins in North Africa, Mess is very in tune with the importance of 24-hour marination of meats. This recipe is very Moroccan, with its lime, turmeric, olive oil, and oregano.

Again, Mess learned much of this from his mom, but it is reinforced by my beliefs about spices and their importance for health.

To get the real impact of this recipe, be sure to prep the chicken *ONE* day before with Mess's magic marinade! The marinade is my favorite part of the recipe, because it is loaded with antioxidant-rich, anti-inflammatory turmeric and vitamin C-packed lime juice. The ingredients of this recipe have immunity- boosting properties and spices that help aid tired, sore muscles and joints.

One note: I couldn't get him to budge on the Lillie's BBQ sauce. He insisted. But other than that, it's a very effective marinade in terms of antioxidant power! I can't win them all! *LOL!*

Also, buckwheat is a great alternative to traditional wheat pasta and is also gluten-free. It has a different taste, but one that most kids will catch on to! Explain that whole grains and seeds (buckwheat is actually a seed derived from the rhubarb plant) and the "brown carbs" are better for them, because they are more complex sugars, and it takes the body a while to break them down, thus giving more energy to the body! So many delicious items in this very hearty meal. The sesame oil adds a delicious kick! Great after a long, hard workout or after a long week of hard training.

Serves 4

Nutrition:

Calories Per Serving: 310

Sodium: 960mg

Fat: 18g

Sugar: 5.6g

Carbohydrates: 17.8g

Protein: 19g

Ingredients:

4 4-ounce organic chicken breasts

The Marinade (prepare the day before; let sit 12-24 hours)

4 tablespoons olive oil

4 tablespoon lime juice

4 tablespoons Lillie's sweet smoky BBQ sauce (this is the product we used; choose any BBQ sauce you like)

1 tablespoon oregano

1 tablespoon onion powder

1 tablespoon turmeric

1 teaspoon salt

1 teaspoon pepper

1/4 cup water

For the soba:

4 ounces uncooked organic buckwheat soba

1 tablespoon sesame oil

1 teaspoon low-sodium soy sauce

1/4 cup chopped green onion (save a little for the topping)

Pepper to taste

1 green pepper sliced longways

1/8 cup water

Steps:

1. Start the marinade process by whisking together ingredients well in a large bowl.
2. Cut and clean chicken then slice chicken into fine pieces.
3. Place the chicken pieces one by one into the bowl of marinade and cover with plastic wrap. Let sit a minimum 12 hours for marination, and up to 24 hours, if possible, for maximum deep-marinating benefit.
4. 24 hours later..., start the soba.... Boil soba noodles for 5 minutes. Drain noodles.
5. In a large pre-heated sauté pan, add the marinated chicken and cook on medium heat for two minutes. Then flip and cook for two minutes on the other side.
6. With a plastic spatula, chop the meat into smaller pieces as you cook. When it's warm through, add the green onions (except for a tablespoon) and pepper with 1/8 cup water. Cook on medium-low for five more minutes.
7. Turn off heat. Add to the sesame oil and soy sauce. Mix well.
8. Serve the chicken over the soba noodles! Sprinkle with the extra green onion. Bon appétit!

Wild Orange Roughy, Sauerkraut, and Brussels Sprouts

Wild orange roughy is a fish I was introduced to back in my bodybuilding days. It has a distinct sweet flavor, and when paired with the vinegar savory sauerkraut, you won't believe the taste! It's loaded with heart-healthy fat, protein, and memory-enhancing omega-3 fatty acids. You do not *have;* to use orange roughy; there are other wild white fish options that will go just as well with this recipe.

Mess and I selected sauerkraut for this cookbook for many reasons. In the Alsatian region, where Mess is from, sauerkraut is a well-known staple. People from around the world go to Strasbourg to eat the sauerkraut. After all, Strasbourg sits right on the French and German border, so there is a huge German influence on the food of Alsace.

Traditional sauerkraut dishes are accompanied by pork, sausage, or other meat. We substituted the meat and pork for a white fish, which we believe to be more functional for athletes and a healthier choice. You may also use other white fish like halibut or cod.

I specifically love sauerkraut for gymnasts because of the rich amounts of vitamins, minerals, fiber, and probiotics. Brussels sprouts are also a part of this very nutrient-dense cabbage family, so why not enjoy them together? Get ready for some delightful smells in your kitchen!

Tools:

    ✳ A strainer (we have one in our store, www.betsymcnally.com)

Serves 2-4

Nutrition:

Calories Per Serving: 284

Sodium: 580

Fat: 16.5g

Carbohydrates: 13g

Sugar: 5g

Protein: 18g

Ingredients

1-1.2 **pounds** sauerkraut

1-1/2 **cups** Brussels sprouts

2-1/2 **ounces** yellow onion (about 1/4 large yellow onion)

2 **tablespoons + 1 teaspoon** olive oil

1 **teaspoon** nutmeg

1 **teaspoon** salt

A **few pinches** of pepper

1/4 **cup** dry white wine

1 **teaspoon** coconut oil

4 orange roughy filets, seasons with **dash** of sea salt and pepper

Lemon and bean sprouts for decoration.

Steps:

1. Remove the sauerkraut and rinse thoroughly in a strainer.
2. Wash Brussels sprouts thoroughly.
3. Slice the onion and Brussels sprouts in half.
4. Place the washed sauerkraut, onion, 2 tablespoons of olive oil, and salt in a large pot over medium heat.
5. Add a few pinches of black pepper. Cover and cook over medium heat for 10 minutes.

6. While this is cooking, steam the Brussels sprouts in a steamer, if you have one. (If you don't have a steamer, boil the Brussels sprouts 10 minutes.)

7. After 10 minutes of cooking the sauerkraut on medium heat, add the wine and lower the heat to medium-low. Stir and cover. Let cook for 30 minutes. (You don't want to cook too long, because it will kill a lot of the minerals, vitamins, and probiotics/good bacteria.)

8. Remove the brussels sprouts and place in a pan with a teaspoon of olive oil. Stir fry over medium heat until crispy.

9. Wash your fish and add a dash of sea salt and pepper.

10. Heat coconut oil in a sauté pan. After oil melts, gently add the fish. Cook five minutes each side or until desired texture.

11. Place the fish on a plate, add the sauerkraut, brussels sprouts and other garnish, and Bon Appétit!

Betsy's Famous Rainbow Veggie Bake

Do *you* Remember ROY G BIV?

Of course, we all learned the colors of the rainbow in school and the order in which they appear. They even taught us a guy's name to help us remember the order of the spectrum: ROY G BIV: Red, Orange, Yellow, Green, Blue, Indigo, and Violet. All of these colors together make the rainbow.

Veggies are sometimes challenging for kids to eat, but this "rainbow" effect will most likely give your kids' *eyes* something to love it, at least! Most kids love how pretty this dish is, and then when they taste it, they love it even more.

This recipe is fairly simple. You can also choose veggies that go best with your family's palette. In our rainbow, I'm including also white veggies (onions and garlic) for their powerful compounds, allium and quercetin! White is what we see when all the wavelengths of light are reflected off an object!

This is a great recipe to take to a summer pool party or when hosting an athletic gathering. The kids love the color and are more willing to try. The added pumpkin seeds and cheese also give it a "lasagna" effect! Here are the veggies I selected for the Rainbow Bake, and why!

Red: Tomatoes; packed with vitamin C and lycopene, which help prevent heart disease, are immunity boosting, and promote collagen and muscle growth.

Orange: Orange Peppers; beta-carotene, vitamin C, lycopene, and calcium. Orange veggies are known for their aid in inflammation; also, promoting collagen growth for healthy bones and muscles.

Yellow: Yellow Squash is packed with flavonoids, vitamin C, beta-carotene. These compounds help with eyes, joints, and bones.

Green: Broccoli and Green Peppers; folate, vitamin C, fiber, calcium, and magnesium. Broccoli is great for digestion, boosting immunity, and strengthening bones.

Blue: Red/Purple Kale; packed with lutein, vitamin C, quercetin—all known for helping immunity, skin, and eye health. The powerful antioxidant anthocyanin is known to boost immunity, improve calcium absorption, and stop the growth cancer cells.

Indigo: Red Cabbage, a cruciferous vegetable potent with probiotics and fiber, is instrumental in helping digestion and helping with constipation and other gastrointestinal issues.

Violet: Purple Cauliflower; also packed with anthocyanin, folate, calcium, and selenium, all amazing vitamins and minerals for immunity, strong bones, and body function on a cellular level.

White: Garlic and Onions. Some of the most potent foods on the planet are white vegetables and roots. They are filled with beta-glucans, which boost immunity and reduce the risk of cancers. They also contain quercetin, a flavonoid that reduces inflammation and helps prevent infections. Lastly, the powerful plants that come from the allium species (garlic, leeks, onions) are all known for fighting tumors and fending off fungus.

Honorable Mention: the Topping! Parmesan cheese, olive oil, pumpkin seeds: lots of healthy fat, calcium, and crunch for some fun!

Serves 6

Prep Time: 30 minutes

Bake time: 1 hour

Tools:

 ✳ A 9-inch glass baking dish.

Nutrition:

Calories Per Serving: 268

Sodium: 208 mg

Fat: 7g

Sugar: 9g

Carbohydrates: 17g

Protein: 6g

Ingredients—Marinade:

4 tablespoons olive oil

3 tablespoons water

1 clove of garlic minced

1 teaspoon lemon juice

2 tablespoons pumpkin seeds

1 tablespoon honey

1 teaspoon pepper

1 tablespoon low-sodium soy sauce

1/3 cup shredded parmesan cheese

Ingredients—The Rainbow:

2 tomatoes sliced

1-1/2 orange peppers sliced

1 yellow squash sliced

2 cups chopped broccoli crowns

1 green pepper chopped

2 cups chopped red/purple kale

1 cup red/purple cabbage chopped

1 cup chopped purple cauliflower

1/4 cup chopped onion

Steps:

1. Preheat oven to 410 degrees
2. Spray the bottom of 9-inch glass pan with cooking spray.
3. Start marinade by mincing your garlic.
4. Then, in a mixing bowl, add 4 tablespoons of olive oil, water, lemon, the minced garlic, soy sauce, honey, and pepper. Whisk together well. Set aside.
5. To start the Rainbow, clean all of your vegetables thoroughly. With a knife, slice each vegetable in the appropriate size and shape to your liking. For the kale, chop into 1-inch-square pieces to become very crunchy. (I go for thinner slices of each vegetable, but it really doesn't matter how you slice them.)
6. Arrange the veggies in lines in the glass dish. Be creative, but make sure you start with Red then Orange, Yellow, Green, Blue, Indigo, Violet, and White, in that order. We want to stay true to ROY G BIV!
7. After lining the veggies in the baking dish, pour the marinade over the veggies, either with a spoon or a measuring cup. Be sure to distribute as evenly as possible.
8. Bake at 410 degrees for 50 minutes.
9. After 50 minutes, remove the veggie pan and top with parmesan cheese and pumpkin seeds.
10. Broil for 5-10 minutes or until crispy!

Enjoy!

Tomato Farcie

This dish is a classic from the Laouar home. Mess's mother made this dish with beef, and he recalls fondly his eating this as a child. This recipe is very well known and eaten frequently in France. Mess's mother made it because he didn't like tomatoes, but she knew how healthy tomatoes were. This was one of the only ways he would eat them!

Functionally speaking, tomatoes are known for their heart-healthy compounds like lutein, lycopene, and vitamin C—all excellent nutrients for eye health, immunity, and cardiovascular health.

We made it a bit healthier with some organic turkey, anti-inflammatory turmeric, and heart-healthy olive oil. It's a delicious dish filled with veggies, complex carbs, and proteins, all essential for a post-workout meal! This is a fun one also for the whole family to make, The kids like "coring" the zucchini!

Tools:

* A Kitchen Aide and fan attachment (available in our store, www.betsymcnally.com)
* Apple corer (in our store)
* A Bullet or Ninja (in our store)
* A strainer (in our store)
* Square glass baking dish or other baking dish of choice

Serves 4-6

Nutrition

Calories: 220 per serving

Sodium: 697mg

Fat: 24.9g

Calories: 871

Sugar: 9g

Carbohydrates: 24.9g

Protein: 23 g

Ingredients for the Stuffing and Veggies:

1/4 cup brown rice (dry measure, before cooking)

2 6-inch-long zucchinis

4 large tomatoes

Ingredients for The Turkey:

16 ounces ground organic turkey meat

2 tablespoons olive oil

1 teaspoon turmeric

1 teaspoon pepper

1 teaspoon onion powder

1 teaspoon lemon or lime juice

1 teaspoon fresh chopped parsley

Pinch of salt to taste

Ingredients for the sauce:

1 more tablespoon olive oil

1 tablespoon minced garlic

1 teaspoon lime or lemon juice

1/4 cup parmesan cheese, for topping at the end

Steps:

1. Cut each zucchini into 3 equal, straight pieces. Core the center of each piece. Slice off the tomato tops. Save the pulp of each tomato in a small bowl.
2. Cook brown rice traditionally with water. Set aside to cool.
3. Preheat oven to 350.
4. While the rice is cooking, boil the zucchini pieces, in a pot of water for 10 minutes.
5. After finished boiling, gently remove zucchini from the water with tongs, if possible, place in a strainer, and run cold water over the zucchini pieces to stop the cooking process. We want them to be cooked but also firm and not breaking apart. Let sit in the strainer and cool.
6. Next, place the turkey, olive oil, turmeric, pepper, onion powder, lemon or lime juice, and parsley in the mixer bowl. Then add in the cooled rice. Using the Kitchen Aid Fan attachment, blend all of this together for about 3-4 minutes. Then stop, and let sit a moment.
7. While this is happening, take the insides of the tomato and place in a bullet blender. Add the tablespoon of olive oil, salt and pepper to taste, a squeeze of lemon juice, and a teaspoon of minced garlic. Blend for 5 seconds (we do not want this to get too liquified, but just enough).
8. Spread this sauce evenly across the bottom of glass baking dish.
9. Form the turkey mixture into small, cylinder-shaped rolls. Gently stuff each of them in the cooled zucchinis. Be sure to stuff them all the way through and level off at the top.
10. Stuff remaining turkey into the tomatoes. Any leftovers, you can roll into balls.
11. Place stuffed zucchini, tomatoes, and balls in the baking dish over the sauce in any preferred design.
12. Bake for 30 minutes at 350 degrees.
13. After 30 minutes, remove the baking dish and raise oven temperature to broil. Add a pinch of parmesan cheese over each turkey ball or stuffed turkey veggie.
14. Broil for 10 minutes. Enjoy!

Gratin of Artichokes with Salmon and Boursin

This is a rich one....

If you want a fine-dining experience, this is your choice! Having friends over to dinner? Make this one!

I love this dish because artichokes are loaded with fiber, vitamins, minerals, and vegetable protein, which are all essential for a gymnast. Salmon is packed with brain-healthy omega-3s and protein. This recipe is a little richer and higher in calories because of the French favorite, Boursin cheese. However, it's worth it because of all the amazing health benefits of the dish.

By the way, can I tell you that I *never even tasted* an artichoke until I met my husband. Mess says he could write an entire cookbook about artichokes He grew up eating them frequently, and they are very popular in France.

He taught me how to cook them, peel the leaves, dip them into an amazing mustard vinaigrette sauce, and scrape off the skin with my teeth. Then, how to eat the most important part: the heart at the bottom of the plant.

Artichokes are one of the healthiest foods on the planet, packed with folate, vitamin K, and fiber. They are definitely one of my superfoods, featured in part three of this book, so check out all the benefits they provide for our athletes.

Tools:

 ★ A baking dish or casserole

Serves 4-6

Prep time: 30minutes

Cook Time: 30 minutes

Nutrition:

> Calories Per Serving: 289
> Sodium: 500mg
> Fat: 18g
> Carbohydrates: 7g
> Sugar: 1g
> Protein: 25g

Ingredients

> **2 12-ounce** jars of marinated, quartered artichoke hearts. (Note: we use the brand Delallo, which are marinated in vinegar.)
>
> **8 ounces** wild salmon
>
> **3 cups** of spinach
>
> **1 5.2-ounce box** Boursin cheese
>
> **1 tablespoon** olive oil
>
> **1 teaspoon** pepper

Steps:

1. Preheat oven to 350 degrees.
2. Optional: If you like a less vinegar taste and use hearts pre-packed in vinegar, rinse the artichokes in cold water. Then boil the artichokes for 10 minutes with a little salt. Let them dry for a few minutes afterward. This will make the artichokes softer and remove a lot of the vinegar taste. You can also boil and use your own fresh artichoke hearts, as well.
3. If using jar, drain the artichokes well.

4. Sauté spinach 3 minutes with olive oil over medium heat. Set aside let cool.
5. Filet salmon in half, but don't open completely. ("Cut them to open like a book," Mess says.)
6. Put two tablespoons of Boursin inside the salmon, spreading it evenly.
7. Add the spinach on top, of cheese, then close the salmon well.
8. Slice the salmon evenly into 1-inch pieces down the length of the filet.
9. Prepare a baking dish with one tablespoon of olive oil. Add the salmon pieces to the baking dish longways.
10. Around the salmon, place the drained artichokes. Spread the rest of the Boursin cheese on and around the salmon and artichokes. Add the pepper.
11. Bake at 350 for 25 minutes.
12. After 25 minutes, increase the temperature to broil. Broil an additional 5 minutes, to give a crusty topping. Bon Appétit!

Betsy's Thoughts: Being the Parent of a Picky Eater–Lenny Laouar

PREGNANCY CAME AS A surprise to me. At thirty-nine years old, I never thought I would get pregnant, so when I got the surprise news that I was pregnant, I was overjoyed, happy, excited. It was a whirlwind.

You never expect that something will go wrong your pregnancy or that a doctor will tell you that something is very wrong with your child in the womb. Our doctors told us early on that our child was measuring abnormally small and there was something wrong with our baby. He was SGA, or small for gestational age, and not growing at a normal rate.

The pregnancy was long, I was on bed rest and watched by French nurses and their staff around the clock to check, to see if the baby was moving.

When my son was born at 2-1/2 pounds on May 19, 2014 in Strasbourg, France, I had no idea what my life would be like in the years to come. I had an emergency C-section with general anesthesia. It was the scariest moment of my life...

My son was whisked away to the Intensive Care Unit, and he stayed there, linked up to machines, for the next seventeen days, and in the hospital for the next two months....

I had no idea that my very frail son would struggle with food. I had no idea he would be born with two holes in his heart and a heart defect. I had no idea he would need emergency hernia surgery when he was just thirty-nine weeks old.

I had no idea that he would be diagnosed with nonverbal autism, or ASD.

I had no idea that he would have eating aversions and not eat solid food.

I had no idea he would struggle with acid reflux until he was two years old, gagging on food, refusing to eat, and drinking a bottle until he was five (currently, he still does).

All of these things came as a surprise to me as my child truly struggled for the first three years of his life. Lenny is now almost five years old, and we now have him eating some solid food.

He is not talking yet, but he is communicating more, and his artistic side is an enjoyable part of his personality. He is very sensory, he loves music and art, and he communicates through a lot of laughing and yelling, screaming, flapping, and movement.

If you've ever known *one* child with autism, then you know *one* child with autism.

What does that mean? That means all children with autism are different.

They all have different struggles and ticks, things that get them upset or make them wild or to which they react differently than "normal" kids. Many autistic kids have special gifts. They make us see the world in a way we never imagined. No one truly understands autism until they live with it every day.

As a parent of a child with autism, I have learned to be really patient and flexible with how we feed our son. He will vomit or gag on food. He will chew up food and spit it out, or he will throw food. Currently, that is the phase we are in: throwing food....

In the early years, we tried everything including food therapists and every kind of texture possible. The therapists would just keep pushing us to try new foods, and we were like, "Yeah, *right!* He will never eat that..." And, normally, he wouldn't eat it.

The truth is, over time, he just decided to start eating. First, it was powdered, textured foods that turned more solid (crushed cookies).

Over time, we became frustrated, because we would spend hours preparing puréed foods in hopes we would find something he actually liked. We tried everything, from puréeing mixtures of yogurt, seeds, and green vegetables. We even puréed beef, salmon, and chicken, hoping to get nutrients, healthy fats, and carbs into his little body. You also have to remember that Lenny wasn't even on the growth chart. He was in the .05 percentile for weight.

It's been a long road. We have done what we have to do to get nutrients into our son. My point in telling you the story is, if you have a picky eater, please don't think we don't understand, because we do. Please don't think we expect your kids to stop eating how they are eating and adapt to a clean eating regime, if they are eating processed foods.

I love it when I begin working with a client and they say, "Betsy, you don't understand. I have a picky eater!"

After hearing them out (I am empathetic and compassionate, because I am in their same boat), I explain to them that yes, in fact, I do *GET IT*. I'm living it every day with you.

The good news is that Lenny has just recently started eating more solid food, like salmon and chicken and even pizza, but it took us a long time, and we never would've gotten there if we hadn't tried, weren't patient, and let this issue defeat us.

You have to try, and you have to try again and again and again. I can't tell you how many times I've helped to completely change an athlete's palate, just by switching up different combinations of foods or putting them in different salads or shakes or recipes. That is what this book is all about.

You have to get creative and you can't be defeated.

My advice: Don't ever say, "I can't do this," or, "This will never change," because, if you have that mentality, you're right: the child will never change.

I have seen miracles happen with children and their nutritional choices. Trust me: I've had kids who would never eat vegetables turn into vegetable lovers. I've had kids who would never eat fish now love fish.

A lot of the recipes in this book will have foods that may seem strange, different, or in weird combinations. Always give a food three or four times before throwing in the towel. We are doing this with you, picky eaters!

I'm telling you my story because I am the mom of a picky eater, too!

Lenny Eats

"*Quand je regarde mes enfants grandir, j'oublie que ma vie s'accélère*"

(When I watch my kids grow, I forget my life is speeding up)

—*Chef Mess*

ལༀལༀལༀལༀལༀ

Mess's thoughts:

We forget about our own aging as we watch our children. Take care of your body as you age through proper nutrition.

VITAMIN-DENSE AND DECADENT DESSERTS

Green Ice Cream

What athlete doesn't love ice cream? Rather, what human doesn't love ice cream? Well, this delicious version of ice cream is not only refreshing and yummy, it's also packed with vitamins and minerals and anti-inflammatory properties.

I recommend serving this tasty "pretend" ice cream on a hot day or right after practice in summer, as it is loaded with protein, vitamins C and K for excellent blood flow, antioxidants in the form of berries, and potassium and magnesium to replenish electrolytes after a long, hard practice. This dessert is perfect for any child who will simply *not* eat green veggies. Sneaking them in is such a dream come true!

In order to make this recipe, you need to follow directions closely to get the right texture and melting point to make real ice cream! We recommend using spherical molds, but you can also use ice cube molds that are round and spherical.

Serves: 4-6 standard servings or 10-18 small servings;, depending on size of your mold

Tools

* Silicon molds or ice cube trays. We used Baker Depot Bakeware Set Silicone Molds (in our online store, www.betsymcnally.com)
* A Nutri Bullet, to completely blend all green pieces

Cook Time: 15 minutes to prepare, 3 hours to freeze, 1 hour to thaw

Nutrition:

Calories Per Single Serving: 50-80, depending on mold/cube size

Sodium: 24 mg

Fat: 1.1g

Sugar: 3.9g

Carbohydrates: 5.6 g

Protein 5 g

Ingredients:

1/2 banana

1 cup almond milk

1 cup strawberries

2 cups kale

1 tablespoon honey

1/2 cup Greek yogurt

For topping:

1/4 cup fresh raspberries or blueberries

Sprinkle of cocoa powder

Steps:

1. Place all of the ingredients into a Nutri Bullet blender. Blend until smooth pour.
2. Pour mixture evenly into the silicon molds/ice cube holder.
3. Let freeze until solid (about two to three hours)

To serve:

4. IMPORTANT: One hour before you would like to eat the ice cream, remove from freezer and let sit at room temperature, to develop a soft, edible texture. You will not be able to remove the ice cream cubes until they are soft.
5. Sprinkle with dark cocoa powder and garnish with fresh berries.

Sweet Potato Crème Brûlée

For this recipe, you will need to prepare and take time! You also need some special tools, so keep that in mind before you try this! It is a very challenging recipe to make, but a fun take-off on your traditional French crème brûlée.

Mess and I worked very hard on this recipe to create just the right texture and temperature for the best possible outcome! Sweet potatoes are a wonderful addition to any gymnast's diet because of their mood-enhancing effects, fiber, vitamin A for skin and eyes, and most importantly the slow breakdown of the vegetable for sustained energy.

The sweet potato is probably one my favorite energy-boosting foods! One of the most perfect complex carbohydrates, it regulates blood sugar and gives long-lasting, sustainable energy.

Loaded with antioxidants, magnesium, and potassium, sweet potatoes are great brain foods, too! It also helps to release serotonin (our feel-good hormone!). This recipe is the perfect dessert or mid-afternoon snack for any athlete who wants to not only receive the benefits of this amazing vegetable, but who also likes a sweet treat!

When I lived in France, I had a really hard time finding sweet potatoes. They were expensive and rare in the grocery stores. As I mentioned in the beginning of this book, I loved the grocery stores overall, but many of the staples I was used to seeing in the U.S. were absent, specifically sweet potatoes. Sweet potatoes are probably one of the most important foods for athletes, because they are complex carbohydrates, which gives steady energy without affecting blood sugar.

By the way, this recipe was fun for me and Mess to create. If you can get a torch to make the crusty top, it's definitely well worth it! Of course, crème brûlée is a common dessert in France, so we merged out ideas together to create this delicious dessert. It is challenging to make but you'll love it!

Tools:

* 4 Ramekins (You can find ours in the online store, www.betsymcnally.com)
* Hand mixer (we used a Kitchen Aide, available in our store) ***DO NOT use a Bullet or a blender: this is very important and has to do with air flow within the mixture.***
* Large pan 3-inches deep that can fit into the oven (We use a 3" Full-Size Anti-Jam Steam Pan, also in our store)
* Mesh hand strainer (we used an 8-inch, also in our store)
* Mini Hand Torch (we used Sondiko Culinary Torch, in our store)

Prep Time: 30 minutes

Serves 4

Nutrition

Calories Per Serving: 146
Sodium: 54 mg
Fat: 7g
Sugar: 8.8g
Carbohydrates: 15.8
Protein: 5.6 g

Ingredients

1 6-ounce sweet potato

4 egg yolks

1 tablespoon whipping cream

½-1 cup milk (amount depends on height of your sweet potatoes in the pot, as explained in steps below)

1 teaspoon white sugar

1 tablespoon raw brown sugar

Steps:

1. Preheat the oven to 325 degrees.
2. Peel the sweet potato. Then slice sweet potato into very thin, 1/8--inch slices.
3. Place slices in a pot with enough milk to cover the sweet potatoes but not above the level of the slices. (We don't want to "drown" the sweet potatoes, but rather cook and soak them.)
4. Over medium heat, cook the milk and sweet potato for 20 minutes. Do not boil. Check often, and turn the sweet potatoes until tender—hey should break with a fork.
5. While the potatoes are cooking, whisk together the eggs and 1 teaspoon of sugar. Beat intensely for about three minutes, until the mix becomes a clear white.
6. Remove sweet potato mix from the stove. Using your hand mixer (*again: do not use a blender,* because the heat will cause an explosive response), mix well until smooth.
7. Strain sweet potato mixture into another bowl. Add the whipped cream and whisk for one minute until mixed well.
8. Place ramekins on the Anti-Jam 3-inch-deep steam pan.
9. Fill ramekins with the sweet potato-cream mix into. Do not fill to the very top of the ramekin. Leave about 1/4 of an inch at the top.
10. ATTENTION: this part is very important, delicate, and challenging! *SLOWLY* add lukewarm water to the pan (not in, just around the ramekins) until just below the level of the top of the ramekin. BE CAREFUL! Do not allow water inside the ramekins! (This ensures the sweet potato crème cooks properly and the ramekin doesn't burn; it creates a vapor—a French technique!)

11. Carefully place the pan with the water and the ramekins in the oven. Preferably cook in a convection oven, if you have that option. If not, it is okay. Bake for 25 minutes.

12. Remove the pan slowly don't forget: you have *HOT* water in the pan! Be very careful! Place on a heat-resistant surface and let sit for 20 minutes.

13. Carefully remove the ramekins and put them in the refrigerator for two hours.

14. Make a thin layer of raw brown sugar in equal amounts on each ramekin, and spread over the top.

15. Using your torch, start to heat the top of each ramekin by moving the torch in circles, so the fire disperses itself evenly on top, creating a crunchy, brûlée top to your liking.

16. Wait a minute before eating! Enjoy

Green Machine Mini-Cakes

It's St. Patrick's Day all year with this delicious spinach cake. Don't tell your kiddos what's in here. Make it and let them try it. I bet they will never guess it's loaded with vitamins, minerals, antioxidants, and healthy fats that will help power them through their next training session.

Mess and I had to really work hard on this recipe several times to get it perfect. Be sure you use the correct amount of coconut oil to get the ideal texture. (Measure it as liquid, not solid.)

You may have to practice a couple times to get the eggs perfect, as well. You must use your electric mixer to create a perfect egg density for this recipe. Again, once you get the texture right, you can't beat this cake for holidays, Christmas, St. Patrick's Day, or even a summer get-together. It's such a delicious and vitamin-packed treat!

Tools:

* A Nutri Bullet or Ninja (in our store, www.betsymcnally.com)
* A Kitchen Aide or electric mixer with whisk for the whipping of the eggs (also in our store)
* 2 small cake baking pans, 5" x 2" (available in our store and highly recommended)

Makes 2-4 servings

NOTE: This recipe is made specifically for mini-cakes You can definitely double the recipe and use a bigger baking pan however the cooking time may increase.

Nutrition:

Calories Per Serving: 400

Sodium: 218mg

Fat: 23.9g

Sugar: 3.5g

Carbohydrate: 40 g

Protein 15g

Ingredients:

4 eggs

1/4 cup almond milk

3/4 cup fresh raspberries

2-1/3 cups or **2.5 ounces** fresh spinach leaves

1/2 cup coconut flour

2 tablespoons coconut oil (melted, liquid state)

Pinch of salt

1/8 cup raw turbinado cane sugar

1 teaspoon baking powder

Steps

1. Take eggs out of refrigerator 1 hour before making the recipe.
2. Preheat oven to 355
3. Melt the coconut oil in a small microwave-safe dish or cup. It melts extremely quickly so you will only need a few seconds in the microwave to melt. Let cool but stay melted/liquid.
4. Place into the Bullet/blender the spinach, raspberries, and almond milk. Blend until smooth (liquified).

5. In a big bowl, beat the eggs vigorously on the highest speed with your Kitchen Aide whisk attachment. (The eggs should become dense, like a mousse.)

6. Add the sugar and continue to beat for five minutes. The mixture will become almost white in color and thick/dense. MAKE SURE the eggs are dense and almost mousse-like before you stop mixing.

7. After it reaches this state (around 5-7. minutes), stop the blender and grab a spatula. Add the spinach, raspberry and almond milk mix into the egg mixture.

8. Then add in the melted coconut, the coconut flour, the pinch of salt, and baking powder. *Do not whisk* this together. Using a spatula, fold the batter SLOWLY in a circular motion. Make sure the liquid on top is well-mixed, but don't mix too quickly. There will be some chunks of flour—that's fine. Mix for a few minutes but again, do not over mix.

9. Spray the mini-pans with a non-stick spray and place half the batter in each of the pans.

10. Bake at 355 for 30 minutes or until cooked through.

11. Let cool thoroughly before removing!

Your kids won't believe there is spinach in here!

Homemade Double-Dark Chocolate Pudding

At 4 p.m. in France you will find most people taking their "goûter," pronounced *"gutay"* for us English-speaking folk! It's the afternoon snack in France. This is a coffee break or what the British call "tea time." In France, it is traditional to have a snack, something sweet, and an espresso or coffee. I learned this delicious tradition when living in Europe. It satisfies a sweet tooth and, when eaten in moderation, will have no effect on your waistline. Now, I partake in the goûter every day, thanks to my French hubby.

By the way, this chocolate pudding is the perfect goûter. Mess calls it one his personal favorites in the cookbook. I love it because dark chocolate is an amazing antioxidant and heart-healthy treat. It helps boost serotonin, which elevates mood. Read more about the effects of dark chocolate in the third section of this book (Betsy's Superfoods for Gymnast). I love a happy gymnast, and most gymnasts will love this snack. You won't be disappointment with this delicious treat.

Tools:

* ✶ 3-4 small dessert glasses

Serves 3-4

Nutrition

Calories Per Serving: 350
Sodium: 50mg
Fat: 25g
Sugar: 17g
Carbohydrates: 26g
Protein: 4.3 g

Ingredients

4 teaspoons cornstarch

2 teaspoons 100% dark cocoa powder

3 tablespoons raw (turbinado) brown sugar

1/4 cup whipping cream

1-2/3 cup coconut milk

1 teaspoon vanilla extract

1/3 cup dark chocolate chips 68 percent minimum

2 tablespoons crushed hazelnuts, walnuts or almonds for topping

Steps

1. In a mixing bowl, add cornstarch, chocolate powder, and sugar with 1/2 cup coconut milk. With a whisk, mix well.
2. In a pot over medium-high heat, add the cream and the rest of the coconut milk and stir. Add the chocolate mixture immediately, using a whisk, and mix until boiling. It will become thick. Remove from heat when it has achieved a thick texture.
3. After removing from the heat, add the chocolate chips and continue to mix.
4. After thoroughly mixing, immediately pour into the small glasses and let it sit in the refrigerator for 1 hour minimum.
5. When ready to serve, add the sprinkle of nuts and enjoy!

Berry Mousse

All French chefs love to make mousse, my husband of course being one of them. I have watched him make mousse a hundred times, and it never gets old. There is quite a bit of technique to making mousse, and we didn't want to overwhelm our readers, as there are already quite a few technical recipes in this book. But make sure you read the directions closely, as it will affect the texture.

We wanted to make another dessert for the book, and Mess considered making a chocolate mousse, but we thought it would be fun to make a berry mousse.

This is a great light dessert, perfect for a summer barbecue or evening treat on a hot day. It will also be a fun mousse to make at a gymnasts get-together. I have years of experience seeing how gymnasts love baking and cooking together, to bond.

You already know how much I love berries. We have put them in so many forms in this book, so why not try the mousse?

Prep Time: 30 minutes (plus 30 minutes to remove eggs from refrigerator before starting recipe)

Tools

* A Nutri Bullet
* Kitchen Aide Whisk Attachment (both are in our store, www.betsymcnally.com)

Serves 4

Nutrition:

Calories Per Serving: 105

Sodium: 36mg

Fat: 2.8g

Calories: 105

Sugar: 10.9g

Carbohydrates: 14.4g

Protein: 4.1 g

Ingredients:

6 egg whites

1-1/2 tablespoons butter

1/4 cup whipped cream

1 cup strawberries

1/2 cup raspberries

1/4 cup blackberries

2 tablespoons brown turbinado sugar

1 teaspoon brown sugar

1/2 teaspoon cinnamon

1/2 teaspoon vanilla extract

Steps:

1. Remove your eggs from the refrigerator 30 minutes before beginning to cook.
2. Add all fruit to Bullet/blender. Blend for 20 seconds until smooth.

3. To a pot over medium-low heat, add your berries, one teaspoon of sugar, cinnamon, and vanilla. Whisk often as you cook for 30 minutes.

4. Remove and place in a bowl in the refrigerator.

5. In your Kitchen Aide with whisk attachment, add egg whites and 2 tablespoons brown sugar. Whisk together for five minutes on maximum speed. It will become a white mousse.

6. Place mousse and in another large mixing bowl and refrigerate.

7. Clean your mixing bowl and whisk.

8. Dry your mixing bowl and place it in the freezer for two minutes.

9. After two minutes, remove mixing bowl from freezer and add the heavy cream. Whisk with the Kitchen Aide/mixer for one minute at high speed.

10. Remove the egg mixture and the fruit mixture from refrigerator. Add both of these into the bowl with the eggs.

11. IMPORTANT: Use a spatula for the next important sequence. *Do not just mix this all together.* Use spatula to mix around the edges of the bowl in a circle, then slice in half. Do this slowly and delicately. Make a half circle then cut the circle in half, down the center of the mixture. Do this for a minute. (This technique allows air to go inside the mix, as we are trying to create a mousse-like substance.) Do this for one minute. It is okay if there are white pieces left in the mix.

12. Place the mousse in a smaller bowl and cover **OR** place into individual glass dessert serving dishes.

13. Cover with plastic wrap and refrigerate for a minimum of 2 hours before eating! *YUM!*

Bon Voyage Adult & Virgin Energy-Boosting Pineapple Shake!

YOU MADE IT TO THE END OF THE RECIPES!

WOOH HOO!

Need this about now? Lol!

Yes, this is a cookbook for gymnasts and athletes, but don't think we would leave you out! We kept in *one* libation for the adults in the house! You deserve it!

I was thinking about *you* relaxing on a beach, drinking this delicious green pineapple shake... After all the hard work you do for your athletes and kids, driving them to and from practice, coaching the long hours, putting in the time as a support for your family or your teams.

If you have read this book cover to cover, then you know I'm not a fan of sports drinks for our gymnasts (and most athletes), especially when we can literally make our own energy and electrolyte-boosting drinks.

This shake can be made "virgin style" for your kiddos or "adult style" for you. It's actually the perfect energy-boosting drink post-workout or after a long swim in the island ocean you are dreaming of.

The shake is filled with energy-boosting vitamin B-6, enzymes for digestion, vitamin C for immunity, and it is collagen-building. It's also packed with hydrating electrolytes and antioxidants, to fend off free radicals and promote energy and health. I had one the last night of creating this book, and it really gave me a ton of energy!

For the kids: Leave out the white rum!

For the adults... add it in (I'm not counting how many shots!) Bon voyage!

Makes 2 Shakes

Tools:

* Blender or Bullet (available in our store, www.betsymcnally.com)

Nutrition:

Calories Per Serving: 198   Sodium: 414mg

Fat: 4.9g   Calories: 198

Sugar: 21.3g   Carbohydrates: 32.9g

Protein: 14g

Ingredients:

1 cup ice (optional but recommended)

3 cups coconut water

2 cups kale or spinach

1 tablespoon chia seeds

1 cup fresh pineapple

1 teaspoon raw honey

1/2 cup plain organic Greek yogurt

For the adults: **1 shot** white rum

If you are a real island fan and need that feeling of being in the sun, add **a pinch** of dehydrated shredded coconut, which adds a bit of monounsaturated heart healthy fat!

Steps:

1. Place everything in a blender and *BLEND*!! YUM!

Betsy's Thoughts: Why Food Is Not the Enemy & Body Image in Our World

THERE ARE A LOT of stigmas attached to gymnastics and food. Years ago, coaches would weigh their athletes and even make them display their weight on a board, so everyone could see (unfortunately, myself included). This was not only humiliating but also was setting up athletes for a lifelong struggle with the scale. I think a lot of coaches now regret having done this and acknowledge it was the wrong choice.

Those days are long gone now. However, today, we have other issues plaguing our young people. With emerging distorted and exaggerated body images displayed in our social media and an image-obsessed world, we have a tough fight for even the "regular" teen who doesn't perform gymnastics. When I say distorted, I'm speaking of images that are displayed all over social media platforms.

The whole mission behind my business and writing this book and my other book is to help our young athletes achieve excellent self-esteem and build confidence through proper nutritional choices. I'm unfortunately fighting against... well... the world.

Currently in our world, there are many misguided images, restrictive diets, and distorted bodies that have been transformed by plastic surgery and fake body parts, over-exercised, filtered, corrected, Photoshopped, and dieted bodies. The stories of eating disorders, body dysmorphia, and low self-esteem are sadly on the rise.

This is where a lot of the restricting comes into play. How do we, as nutrition coaches, help athletes and kids get through this moment, especially kids going through puberty or performing in collegiate or elite sports?

I feel it is my *DUTY* to reach out to these kids, these athletes, these women, and tell them this is all *not true*. These images are *not real*. As a real woman, a fit woman, and an ex-athlete, it's my mission to inspire these young, impressionable athletes to treat their bodies with respect through proper, natural fueling.

If we can teach our young people that food is not the enemy and food is a segue to performance, then we can help the youth of tomorrow.

Food is fuel. It shouldn't be restricted or used for punishment or abused in the form of reward.

Of course, food is also an amazing, beautiful thing to be enjoyed. However, many times athletes are taught to think that food is the enemy, especially with weight-related sports like wrestling, gymnastics, dance, ice-skating, and acrobatics. This issue doesn't just stay with gymnastics. There are several other activities and sports that support this type of thinking and practice. Sometimes, parents and coaches just don't know what to do about it....

Just last week, a parent contacted me to tell me she had been weighing her daughter in daily, because she needed to lose weight. Her daughter was actually gaining weight. *Hmm...* I wonder where the issue is there? One can only assume that, when she is not with Mom, she is going "off the plan." When we are told not to do something, our first response, normally, is to do it! So, how do we deal with this issue? I know most parents and coaches really want the best for their athletes, but how can we do it without presenting food as the enemy?

It's tricky, but it can be done through education, proper modeling as adults, and praising the positive attributes of our athlete's strength. *BALANCE* is crucial in this world. Hopefully, a cookbook like this, loaded with education, will help athletes choose foods that will energize them, and make them feel quicker and tighter, mentally and physically, and more confident. The last thing we want to do to the vulnerable young athlete is teach them a life of restriction. This will backfire. I have seen it so many times.

Remember, I don't advocate excessive eating of processed foods. That is one huge area I focus on: *eliminating* eating processed foods. I can hear readers saying, "Betsy, you say not to restrict, but what about processed foods? You are contradicting yourself!"

My point is how can we have athletes and families live *healthy* lives? Stop eating processed foods, not because they make an athlete overweight or fat, but because they're loaded with sodium, sugar alcohols, colorant, preservatives, and additives—all things a human being should avoid eating or making a consistent diet of. I hope you understand what I'm saying.

I'm not saying you shouldn't ever eat processed foods. That's probably not realistic. What I am saying is be aware of the effects they have on performance and overall health. Focus on eating more of the functional foods and the foods that make you feel better, give you energy, and help with inflammation, and you're going to become a better athlete. The focus needs to be: Eat *more* of *these* foods, and *less* of those foods for performance.

If you can increase education on functional foods, you will feel better and increase your confidence. With confidence, you will increase your performance. Once we help athletes make that connection, we are doing our job.

Empowering athletes to choose what they want to eat and not feel like they need to restrict because of an image or an ad they saw about a diet, or because of something somebody told them about, if they eat that food they will get fat... That's where we need to go.

Education, eating a wide variety of foods, and enjoying everything in balance. Food is not the enemy. It is the key to success.

PART TWO

BETSY'S GYMNASTICS KITCHEN

"*Mieux vaut prévenir que guérir*"

(It is better to prevent than to heal)

—French Proverb

୯୫୯୫୯୫୯୫

Mess's thoughts:

Eat the right foods to prevent sickness....

Functional Oils for Gymnasts

COOKING HEALTHY doesn't have to be boring or tasteless! Gone are the days of deep-frying and sautéing in butter, lard, or trans-fats. Today, there are many cooking oils that also serve a higher purpose for bodies under stress.

These are the top three oils—along with their seeds and fruits—that I love. They're absolutely perfect for gymnasts.

1. **Flaxseed/Flaxseed Oil**

Flaxseeds come from the plant "linum usitatissimum." These seeds, when cold-pressed, are filled with a rich, fatty oil also called linseed oil. This fat is truly amazing as it is filled with heart-healthy fiber and a serious dose of omega-3 and ALA (alpha-linolenic acid), fatty acids the body needs but can't produce on its own.

I love flaxseed oil for gymnasts because it fights inflammation of the joints and bones. It is filled with powerful "lignans," which are compounds that fight infection and viruses. Flaxseed oil helps with both immunity and also infection. Flaxseed oil additionally helps with brain function and keeps female hormones balanced!

Always buy organic and cold-pressed, and make sure you refrigerate this oil after opening. It only stays good for six to eight weeks, because it oxidizes quickly. You can sprinkle the seeds as well!

I recommend one tablespoon a day used in one of these ways:

* Stir into a smoothie
* Use as you would butter on toast, in oatmeal, on sweet potatoes
* Stir the seeds into Greek yogurt or protein shakes, or sprinkle on top of salads

2. Coconut Oil (water and milk, too!)

Coconut is quite possibly the most amazing food on the planet. One reason I love coconut specifically for gymnasts is because of its energy-producing ability. Coconut oil will help gymnasts power through four-to-six-hour workouts with its healthy fat called "medium-chain triglycerides," or MCTs. MCTs are fatty acids the body uses for immediate energy instead of storing it in the fat cells.

Coconut oil is extracted from the meat of the coconut. It's one of my favorite "cure-alls" for gymnasts because of its anti-fungal and antibacterial properties. Rub coconut oil in your hair for extra shine and strength, or on your ripped hands to avoid fungal and bacterial infections.

Use a tablespoon on your toast, corn on the cob, sweet potato, or anywhere you want to spread butter (like popcorn). You can even brush your teeth with coconut oil—it's that powerful!

Other benefits of coconut oil?

* It is rich in healthy fat for skin, nails, and hair
* It is heart-healthy and can lower bad cholesterol
* It is delicious on any food
* You can cook with it!

Moving on to coconut milk....

Coconut milk is found after the meat of the coconut is crushed—usually taken from more mature coconuts. Coconut milk is one of the best substitutes for people who are lactose-intolerant or have allergies to milk or nuts. The milk not only tastes amazing but it is loaded with electrolytes and vitamins and minerals that gymnasts need. It also is filled with those healthy fats we talked about earlier!

Try coconut milk with a little cocoa powder for a great post-workout drink. It has less sugar than a sports drink and supplies you with a similar electrolyte boost of iron, magnesium, copper, and calcium.

Let's not forget about coconut water... or the shreds!

Coconut water is the water inside of the coconut right after cracking. It comes from younger coconuts and is another great substitute for sports drinks. Coconut water is tasty, filled with great minerals and natural sugars, and it's great in green shakes and smoothies. You can also use coconut shreds in your shakes, in yogurt, or sprinkled over toast.

3. **Olive Oil**

Quite possibly the most heart-healthy oil on the planet is olive oil. Olive oil comes from the pressing of their fruit: the olive.

Olives are known as the main staple of the Mediterranean diet. This diet is known all over the world to help lower the risk of cardiovascular and heart disease and help with joint and muscle inflammation. This diet is loaded with tomatoes, grapes, nuts, greens, lean meats, and, of course, lots of olive oil and olives.

But why is olive oil great for gymnasts? First, because of its anti-inflammatory properties: it helps with sore muscles and joints. The ancient Greeks were on to something when they used olive oil as a massage cream for sports injuries and muscle fatigue. Try massaging sore muscles with this miracle oil!

Olives are loaded with skin-loving vitamin E and filled with potent anti-oxidant powers (anti-cancer, anti-disease). Olives are also filled with unsaturated healthy fat and antibacterial properties. You can eat olives by themselves, pair with fruit and cheese, or add to salads. Olive oil keeps your joints lubricated and your immunity strong.

I recommend one to two tablespoons daily for a strong gymnast!

* Use olive oil on salads with balsamic or apple cider vinegar
* Use while sautéing meats, veggies, and eggs
* Make an exfoliating and calming face scrub by adding a squeeze of lemon to a tablespoon of olive oil and sugar

Energy Foods for Gymnasts

EVER FEEL LIKE you have done all of the conditioning in the world and yet you still can't seem to make it through your floor routine? Are you feeling tired after only one hour of your four-hour practice?

The problem may not be in your conditioning regime but rather in the foods you are eating—or NOT eating.

Here are various different reasons that could contribute to a lack of energy:

- ✓ Lack of sleep
- ✓ Too much processed sugar in your diet
- ✓ Not enough water
- ✓ Lack of essential vitamins and minerals that support energy production

Here are some vitamins and minerals you may need to replenish if your energy is lacking:

Magnesium

This mineral is responsible for activating ATP in the body, which is the most fundamental component of energy. It basically "starts our engines." Magnesium provides us not only with energy but also helps activate nerves in the body, aids in muscle soreness and cramping, and relieves constipation. If you are lacking in this mineral, you may be feeling sluggish and slow.

Gymnasts need to make sure they are getting enough magnesium in their diets through foods such as avocados, yogurt, spinach, nuts, and seeds.

Add a spinach salad to your meal plan, and top it with seeds and avocados for a magnesium-rich meal.

Vitamin B12

This vitamin is essential for all gymnasts because it keeps blood cells strong and functioning at their highest level. It's crucial for proper cell metabolism, nerve function, and energy production.

If you are feeling fatigued, try to up your intake of foods rich in vitamin B12. Some great sources of B12 are organic, grass-fed meats; chicken and eggs; wild fish; and... *ewww*, yuck... liver! Think like a Stone-Age cavewoman and return to your meat-eating ways, if you are always tired during practice!

A great way to get B12 into your diet is by eating eggs and chicken for breakfast. Try two egg whites and one whole egg scrambled with 3 ounces of shredded, grilled chicken. Scramble in magnesium-full and fiber-rich spinach for a delicious breakfast omelet.

Often, in my nutrition seminars, I get many questions regarding the extra supplementation of vitamin-B12 shots. Many times, if athletes aren't getting or absorbing enough B12, they will supplement through these shots. As a sports nutritionist, I always recommend you ask your doctor before adding any supplements to your diets not found in "regular food."

Iodine

Iodine is a mineral that helps with the function of our glands, specifically thyroid production. A slow thyroid leads to low energy and sluggishness. Metabolism can be enhanced through foods rich in iodine.

Iodine helps our glands function, which directly affects our energy and metabolism. It's also important for skin and brain health. Some foods rich in iodine are egg yolks, dried prunes, and wild fish such as tuna and halibut, as well as plants from the sea, including seaweed (nori, kombu, and wakame). Sushi, anyone?

In addition, complex carbohydrates (such as oatmeal, brown rice, quinoa, and sweet potatoes) help with energy production and keep blood sugar stable.

More Energy Ideas

TRY THESE FOODS if you are bonking out on your last tumbling pass!

Chia seeds: This ancient food is defined as "strength" in the Mayan language. Add to salads and green shakes, or crunch on these powerful seeds filled with iodine, magnesium, fiber, and essential fatty acids.

Seaweed: It's rich in vitamins and minerals that are non-toxic, non-GMO, and "organic" naturally. Try out seaweed salad and seaweed chips, or eat sushi rolls that are wrapped in nori! I have yet to meet a gymnast who doesn't like sushi with her gal pals!

Pineapple: My favorite energy food of the bunch. Pineapple is filled with magnesium, and digestive and anti-inflammatory compounds. What gymnast doesn't want energy, great digestion, and help for her sore muscles? Pineapple is a gymnast essential! Add it to fruit salads and smoothies, or eat plain for a delicious pre-workout snack!

SUMMER IS OVER! Back to School Nutrition for Gymnasts

WOW! AFTER A GREAT summer of training hard, traveling, swimming, and downtime with family, gymnasts need some refuel time to heal injuries, work on getting stronger, and relax a bit so they can be fresh for the next season ahead.

As summer winds down and school starts back up, schedules return to normal and gymnastics preseason training is about to start. Things get more serious as skills firm up. This is the ideal time to push the endurance training needed for routines and show off those new skills!

During this period of training, it is important to fuel up on foods that help with long-term energy and muscle endurance. Gymnasts also need to eat foods that aid in muscle repair, to stay healthy during the preseason. While you are turning on the routine prep, here are some simple rules to follow during this time:

1. DON'T SKIMP ON BREAKFAST

This is a huge issue with gymnasts! For some reason, many of them don't like to eat breakfast. Think about this: you burn *most* of your calories in the morning and afternoon, before you even get to practice—moving around, walking, going to school, functioning, and living. The body itself needs a lot of calories to survive, breathe, and function even without physical activity. Then add in a four-hour practice at the end of the school day, and if you haven't fueled up properly.... your practice will be a disaster!

Here are my breakfast favorites for gymnasts:

* Oatmeal with honey, almond butter, and chia seeds. Oats are a complex carbohydrate, which means they will fuel your body for hours and hours. Mixed with the healthy fat and protein of almond butter and the power and energy of the chia seeds, you have a perfect gymnast breakfast.
* Two egg whites and one whole egg scrambled on Ezekiel toast with a tablespoon of coconut oil. Ezekiel toast is filled with protein and healthy grains. It is much better alternative to processed white breads. Add in the healthy energy-boosting fat of coconut oil and the protein-filled egg, and you are ready to start the day.

2. PREPARE YOUR LUNCH BEFORE YOU LEAVE FOR THE DAY

Preparation is crucial to successful eating. If you don't prepare, you may find yourself at the vending machine buying junk that won't fuel your tank!

Lunch should include complex carbohydrates, proteins, and greens that will boost energy throughout the day and gymnastics workout. Remember, when you are planning your meals, you have to think about what we you will be doing *hours* in advance.

Here are some of my favorite lunches for gymnasts:

* Ground turkey burger with avocado, green beans, and a sweet potato with coconut oil. Eat ground turkey for protein, sweet potato for its amazing energy source, and coconut oil, which is rich in medium-chain triglycerides, green beans for fiber, and avocado packed with magnesium and healthy fat.
* Quinoa mixed with no-salt seasoning, grilled chicken, broccoli, and olive oil. Quinoa is a healthy grain loaded with protein, broccoli is packed with calcium for bones, and olive oil is heart-healthy. You can't beat the protein in chicken, either, so mix it all up and enjoy this hearty yet healthy lunch.

3. TAKE YOUR PRE-WORKOUT SNACKS SERIOUSLY

Pre-workout snacks are crucial to any gymnastics practice. You will need a quick shot of energy with a bit of protein and some simple, natural sugars to power you through that workout, but nothing too heavy. Rice cakes with toppings are light enough to eat an hour or so before practice but have awesome energy-packed nutrients.

Try my three favorite whole grain rice cake snacks:

* A whole-grain rice cake with natural almond butter or tahini butter, topped with strawberries and honey
* A whole-grain rice cake topped with 1/3 cup cottage cheese, pineapple slices, and a sprinkle of chia seeds or coconut shreds
* A whole-grain rice cake with 1/4 cup hummus, cucumber slices, and dollop of fresh salsa

4. POST-WORKOUT SNACKS ARE ESSENTIAL FOR REFUELING AND REPAIRING

Your post-workout snack is just as important as your pre-workout snack. You need protein to repair muscles and carbohydrates to refuel glycogen stores.

Here are a few of my favorite post-workout snacks for gymnasts during the preseason:

* Green shake with **1/2 cup** Greek yogurt, **1/4 cup** blueberries, **3 cups** of kale, a tablespoon of sliced almonds, **2 cups** of coconut water, and a **drizzle** of honey. Blend before practice, and store in the fridge while you train. This snack is protein-packed with lots of refueling power for those muscles!
* **1/2 cup** of dry edamame or **1/3 cup** of walnuts, **one** organic string cheese, and a **cup** of strawberries. Crunchy, sweet, and packed with healthy fat and protein!

Remember: you should eat this post-workout snack within a half hour of training, then within the next hour after you have your post-workout meal/dinner.

5. MAKE TIME TO EAT DINNER

After a long, hard day, sometimes the last thing we want to do is cook dinner. However, this is where many go wrong. Most turn to fast food, takeout, or other convenience foods due to lack of preparation. Take one day a week to chop veggies and fruits, pre-cook, and store meats in Baggies for grab-and-go additions to salads for your evening meals. Or try simple creation dinners that include eggs and salads.

Your post-workout meal should include another round of complex carbohydrates, like brown rice, lentils, sweet potato, or quinoa, with a healthy dose of protein, like fish, chicken, eggs, or lean beef. Your dinner should also include plenty of green veggies for energy.

Here are my favorite post-workout dinner meals for gymnasts:

* Anything-Goes salad! Take 3 cups of kale or spinach and add 1-2 cups of any veggie you want to the salad. Top that with 4 ounces of lean meat or chicken or fish, and sprinkle on some sunflower seeds with 2 tablespoons of olive oil and vinegar. This salad is filled with anti-inflammatory properties and loaded with vitamins, minerals, and protein!
* Breakfast for dinner! Crack four or five egg whites, and scramble with a cup of spinach and peppers. Add a pinch of fresh parmesan, fold in 1/2 cup of brown rice or quinoa. Add a cup of fruit, and voila! You've got breakfast for dinner! Lots of protein, simple sugar, and yummy for dinner!

Fighting Inflammation with Food

YOU ARE WHAT you eat! No words have been truer for gymnasts. Constant pounding, jumping, hard landings, and four-hour workouts! The last thing a gymnast needs is to aggravate muscles and joints with foods that add to their soreness.

Processed foods that include white sugar and flour, pasta, fried/fatty foods, sodas, and candy all add to the aches and pains an athlete already feels. Inflammation is alive and well in the American diet, and for athletes performing at a high level, the effects can be devastating.

When I was pregnant in 2015/2016, I craved sugary, processed, and fatty foods. Normally, I am a vegetarian and eat a highly anti-inflammatory diet filled with dark leafy greens, fruits, vegetables, healthy omega-3 fats, seeds, and non-processed, sprouted grain breads.

The drastic change in my diet made me ache all over! I felt muscle soreness and tired; my joints and muscles were on fire. I thought at first it was my hormones, but when I returned to my regular diet, the soreness was gone. Why? Because I was eating foods that aggravated and caused inflammation in my muscles and joints on a cellular level.

This could be happening to you, your child, or your athletes (gymnasts). How can we fight this problem? Through proper nutrition and education on which foods to avoid and which foods to eat more of, we can drastically heal our recovery.

Here are my recommendations for foods that calm down joints and muscles:

Omega-3 Fats (Olive oil, Salmon, Flax Seeds, Walnuts)

Omega-3s are crucial for aiding in inflammation. I know, if I don't take my fish oil supplement daily, my knees ache, my Achilles tendons are sore, and I get headaches. Omega-3 fatty acids are not made by the body. They have to be supplemented with the foods we eat.

Think about a car: it can't run without being a "well-oiled up" machine, right? Think of omega-3s as the oil that keeps your joints, muscles, and bones gliding over each other smoothly. So, where can we find these Omega-3s?

Olive oil has quercetin, a compound that aids in blood flow, and helps with endurance, heart health, and cardiovascular activity. Many believe quercetin is helpful in aiding athletic performance and helping with soreness.

Flax seeds have lignans, which are high in fiber and help with cardiovascular health and performance. Incorporate more fatty fish like salmon, which is great for the heart and brain, and drizzle flax seed oil, olive oil, and walnut pieces over salads daily to get the most out of these powerful anti-inflammatories.

Beets

This powerful red vegetable is loaded with "betalain," which is an antioxidant that helps calm inflammation on a cellular level. It is also loaded with potassium and magnesium, both crucial for muscle, joint, and bone health. The powerful, dense, rich, staining red color is very telling of its power on the cells of the body! Slice up a beet, and place it over a kale or spinach salad with a little goat cheese, cucumbers, and your favorite lean meat. Or add it to your favorite kale shake!

Blueberries

Like olive oil and kale, blueberries contain quercetin, that powerful anti-oxidant responsible for increasing blood flow and decreasing inflammation.

Blueberries are also great for the brain and memory! Blueberries have been shown in many studies to stave off free radicals that are trying to destroy our cells. Gymnasts should incorporate two to three servings of fresh berries, including blueberries, in their daily menus. Try them frozen and on top of plain Greek yogurt for a delicious post-workout snack

Kale

Kale is loaded with vitamin K, which is known for its help with blood flow and anti-inflammation. Kale improves cardiovascular and blood health and has lutein for eye health. Kale also contains the powerful antioxidant quercetin. Many gymnasts need to eat kale to help with their athletic performance—but aren't in love with the taste. If you aren't already drinking kale shakes, I highly recommend them. If you don't have an electric blender or NutriBullet, I highly recommend investing in one. You can find one in our store, www.betsymcnally.com!

Sprouted Grain/Ezekiel Bread

Although not an "anti-inflammatory" food per se, it is a great alternative to processed white and wheat breads and will not cause inflammation. Sprouted grain breads are predigested, broken-down grains, so they are easily digested and better for gut function. There is more fiber and protein in Ezekiel bread than regular white bread and some wheat and whole grain breads. There is no sugar or flour (remember: those two things cause inflammation). Ezekiel bread is a much better alternative to processed wraps, tortillas, and breads. Try toasting some sprouted-grain bread and dipping it into olive oil with a little balsamic vinegar for a pre-dinner treat. Or, for breakfast, add a few egg whites to this toasted treat and little coconut oil.

Functional Foods for Gymnasts

IF YOU ARE a competitive gymnast, you most likely do not live a "normal" life. You are training three to five hours per day, rushing from school to the gym to home, trying to cram in homework and some sort of social life. On top of that, your body is tired, sore, and in need of repair, energy, and rehabilitation.

As I travel, speaking at gyms around the country and working with parents and gymnasts daily, I come across the same questions over and over again about nutrition for the competitive gymnast. What I find in common everywhere is that gymnasts are dealing with tired, sore, and broken-down bodies. Gymnasts need *more* functional foods, which are foods that can help with energy, joint and muscle soreness, muscle repair, fatigue, sickness, and fungus.

Here are my top go-to functional foods for gymnasts:

Garlic: For fungus and infections

If you aren't cooking with garlic, it's time to do so! Add a clove into stir fries to spice up fish and chicken. The gyms you are training in are most likely loaded with fungus. Garlic helps to fend off fungus. (Yes, I see warts and athlete's foot all the time!) Put more into your body to fight off infection and to help build immunity against pesky fungal infections, as well as the common cold. Garlic has also been shown to fight off tumor growth.

Turmeric: For inflammation, sore muscles, and immunity

How many times have you said this? "I'm soooooooo sore." Use turmeric, a spice from the ginger family, to spice up chicken, fish, eggs, rice, and vegetable dishes. It's a super-spice, filled with strong antioxidants to fend off inflammation of the joints and muscles. It's also filled with potent compounds that fight off cancer-promoting free radicals, tumors, and fungus.

Berries: For energy and immunity

Potent, energy-giving berries are filled with phytochemicals and vitamins that stave off infection, help with immunity, and fight the common cold. If you aren't incorporating a daily dose of berries, up your intake to a cup a day of blueberries, raspberries, goji berries, and black berries. You can put them in your oatmeal or yogurt, or eat them fresh—just give them a good rinse before you do so! We include many recipes with berries throughout this book, including our favorites: Quinoa and Fruit Salad, Mess's Berry Delicious Waffle, and Berry Mousse.

Pomegranate: For inflammation, energy, and fighting infections

Sore muscles? Need extra energy for workouts? Fighting the common cold? Herein lies one of the most powerful free-radical fighting foods on the planet: the pomegranate seed! It takes a little knack to open one of these luscious fruits, but once you crack it open, enjoy these tasty seeds on salads, in yogurts and cereal, or at the bottom of your water glass! Also check out our Lime-Whipped Greek Yogurt with Pomegranate Crunch in the recipe section. A sure winner!

Greek Yogurt: For intestinal health and muscle repair

Need more protein to repair those muscles after a workout? If you can't get to your grilled chicken fast enough, grab a cup of Greek yogurt. Greek yogurt is an amazing functional food because of the probiotics/healthy bacteria that we all need in our guts for them to function. If you are struggling with gas and/or intestinal or bowel issues, which *no* gymnast wants while flipping around, add a daily dose of Greek yogurt to your meal plan.

Sources of Calcium Other Than Milk?

A GYMNAST NEEDS healthy cell function and strength in muscles and bones to perform optimally.

Calcium is one essential mineral that many parents ask me about. Is it necessary for an athlete to consume a large quantity of milk or even dairy, to get the required daily intake and support strong muscles and bones? Everyone knows that gymnastics is a sport with its fair share of bone fractures. What can we do to prevent these fractures and increase calcium intake without over-consuming dairy?

The truth is, milk is a very controversial topic. You may have heard the saying, "No one should drink cow's milk—except baby cows!" Essentially, this does kind of make sense. Humans are the only animals that drink another animal's milk. Non-organic dairy can be suspect, as many dairy products incorporate the use of antibiotics, genetically-modified organisms, and hormones. Not to mention, milk contains a lot of sugar—or lactose—which a large majority of the population cannot digest.

I do not want to sway the reader into believing one way or another that milk is "bad" or "good." However, I encourage you to do your own research. What I would like to present are the *many* other forms of calcium out there, which are just as effective or better than milk to fuel the athlete.

My favorites options are the cruciferous vegetables below:

Kale

There are 101 mg of calcium in one cup of kale—which is not only a powerful antioxidant but also an anti-inflammatory and delicious in green shakes. Add 3-4 cups to coconut water and mixed berries to a Bullet or Ninja blender, and enjoy a calcium-rich treat!

Bok Choy

Serves up 75 mg calcium per cup of. This is known as Chinese cabbage, loaded with vitamins C, A, and K. It is great for blood flow and cardiovascular health, helping immunity, and strengthening bones. Add to soups and salad or stir fries with a bit of fresh ginger for a powerful anti-oxidant and calcium-loaded meal. Bok choy is also great for intestinal function, to keep our systems moving!

Rapini (Broccoli Rabe)

This is one of my favorites, and if you are Italian, you may be familiar with it! It is popular in traditional Italian dishes. If you are tentative about broccoli, give its cousin a try! There are 100 mg of calcium in one 2/3-cup serving! Steam, or crunch on them raw, or dip into hummus for a delicious afternoon snack.

Okra

Okra is not part of the cruciferous family, but it is a delicious, flowering green veggie! It is a flowering plant that produces edible seed pods or "ladies fingers." They are great sautéed, grilled, or roasted, and used in stews and soups. Amazingly, they are packed with 172 mg of calcium in one cup plus tons of fiber, folate, vitamin C for immunity, and vitamin K for blood. This food is native to more tropical climates, but try it out for a "shake-up" in your regular meal plan. Your bones will thank you!

My other favorite foods loaded with calcium:

* Sunflower seeds (great on salads and in trail mixes), 50 mg calcium per half cup
* Edamame (great roasted or steamed), 98 mg per 1 cup cooked
* White beans, 63 mg per 1/2 cup cooked
* Almonds, 75 mg per ounce
* Oranges, 74 mg per medium-sized portion
* Spinach, 90 mg per 3 cups

Get creative, and try other forms of calcium to keep your cells, muscles, and bones strong and healthy this year! And do some research on milk. There is a lot of information out there—be sure you are well informed.

Gymnast Power Food: *Seeds*

WHEN PREPARING MEAL plans for my gymnasts, I always include seeds in their diets. Seeds are some of the most important components of a diet rich in calcium, magnesium, vitamins, protein, fatty acids, and antioxidants. These are all important for athletes, who need to keep bones and muscles strong.

Below, I've listed my favorite seeds and *why* they are essential to a gymnast's meal plan.

Sesame

This seed is famous for being on hamburger buns, but it actually has health benefits that do more than just sit on top of your burger. Sesame seeds are known for calcium, copper, and magnesium, which are all essential for strong bones and muscle function.

Sesame seeds are also known for their anti-inflammatory effects, which relieve tired and sore muscles. Try tahini butter, a nutty butter made from the seeds of sesame, and spread it on Ezekiel toast or mix it into Greek yogurt for a nutty treat.

A fair warning: tahini does have a bitter taste that many kids won't love at first. Try sweetening it with a little honey to make the experience tasty!

Pumpkin

Halloween may be just around the corner, but there is more to do with the inside of that pumpkin than just throwing out the contents. Like sesame seeds, pumpkin seeds are loaded with magnesium, copper, and calcium, which all aid with strong bone and brain function as well as wound healing.

The seeds are also filled with omega-3 fatty acids, which help with heart and, again, brain health. An interesting fact about pumpkin seeds is research suggests they help with sleep, due to the amino acid tryptophan found in them. After a four-hour practice, a gymnast most definitely needs her sleep!

Chia

These seeds are very popular right now with health-food gurus. Chia means "strength" in the Mayan language. This is an ancient seed. These seeds are known for helping metabolism and energy. They are also loaded with protein, fiber, and omega-3s.

All gymnasts need energy, protein for muscle repair, and healthy fats for joint and brain health. Add these seeds into green kale shakes or on top of yogurt, or use in chicken or fish marinades for a crunchy punch.

Sunflower

It's not just a pretty flower! Inside are some of the most powerful seeds on Earth. These selenium-rich seeds are known for their anti-cancer properties. And their vitamin E works wonders for skin, hair, and nails, and again, they have more magnesium and calcium for bone health.

These seeds can also help with muscle soreness and energy. Sprinkle them on top of salads, or eat in snack mixes with other dried fruits or nuts.

Pomegranate

This beautiful, colorful, and somewhat tough-to-eat fruit is loaded with some of the most powerful and potent anti-oxidants on the planet. Pomegranate destroys free radicals that prey upon healthy cells. The seeds of this fruit are loaded with vitamin C to improve immunity and fend off sickness.

Pomegranate seeds are also heart-healthy and help with blood flow and cartilage repair. Gymnasts are consistently on tight schedules, which compromise their immunity and break down muscle fibers daily. Add pomegranate seeds to salads, in the bottom of a sparkling water drinks, or eat them by the handful for a sweet, juicy snack.

If you are a gymnast, add these seeds to your meal plan! They are not only delicious but also functional, aiding your muscle repair, bone health, energy levels, sleep, and more!

A Gymnast's Guide to Eating Out

EATING CLEAN IS simple if you prepare and understand the main concepts: eat fresh foods—organic, if possible—and eliminate processed, pre-packaged, and boxed foods.

In general, these concepts are easy to follow. But when faced with traveling or little preparation, it can be challenging to eat clean—especially at a restaurant where you have no idea how your food is being prepared. Below, you'll find some ideas for clean eating at restaurants.

Try to limit the "white stuff" and appetizers

Here comes the bread basket and the appetizers! They always look good, but beware. Most of the time, the pre-dinner bread is made from white flour. Most white foods, including white bread, are made with processed sugar. Just be safe, and pass on the bread basket. And if you absolutely must have an appetizer, try a side salad or vegetable plate.

While planning your main meal, look for colors. Instead of white rice, choose brown, quinoa, or lentils. Instead of a white potato, choose a sweet potato. Instead of white bread, go for whole grain or oat breads. Load up on multicolored peppers and colorful veggies, if offered. Try to limit nutritionally void or fried toppings, like croutons, fried onion straws, and excessively oily cheese, which lack fiber and could contain large amounts of trans fat and processed sugar.

Cook it clean

Always make sure your food is grilled, baked, broiled, or boiled. Fried food has been linked to heart disease and many other health problems. Try to eliminate "fried" chicken, onions, and French fries.

Also watch out for words like "covered," "smothered," and "coated": they often describe calorie-dense foods with little nutritional value. When choosing an appetizer, go for lean meats like ahi tuna, or spreads like guacamole or hummus, and fresh shrimp salads or vegetable plates.

When in doubt, always go green

You can never go wrong with a green food: spinach, kale, peppers, green beans, broccoli, Brussels sprouts, and asparagus. If any of these are on the menu, double up on them in place of side items like mac and cheese or a loaded baked potato. Green foods are full of potassium, fiber, and folic acid, which are all great for competitive athletes.

Eat like a cavewoman

If it had a face, swam in the ocean, grew on a tree, or came from the earth, it is probably clean! Eat like a cavewoman!! When dining out, choose foods as close as possible to real, whole foods in their most natural forms. Choose whole grains and salads with berries, fish, grilled chicken, leafy greens, and nuts. Cave people didn't have the option to order deep-fried chicken, onion rings, or barbecue-basted pork loin.

Dressings and condiments on the side

Dressings and condiments add a ton of additives and sodium to otherwise clean meals. Always ask for dressings and sauce on the side, and dip your fork in!

If you need some spice, go for foods with fresh garlic, lemon, and pepper. Also, olive oil is a great dipping sauce with vinegar.

Dessert?

If you absolutely must indulge in dessert, go for coffee with a bit of cream and cinnamon. Hot, mint, or green tea is not only a refreshing choice after a meal, but it also helps with digestion and is loaded with anti-oxidants.

A fresh-fruit dessert is also great, with a dollop of fresh cream, if possible. Many restaurants are flexible and can create a fruit dessert, if asked. When given the choice of processed sugar in a chocolate brownie or the option of natural sugar, like berries or fruit, *always* choose the natural option. After all, most cavemen didn't have the opportunity to bake brownies!

And by the way, if there is a dark-chocolate choice, go for it! Dark chocolate is an amazing antioxidant loaded with powerful elements that help elevate mood, increase healthy blood flow, and fend of free radicals that are destroying or cells.

And don't forget, BALANCE IS CRUCIAL! It is okay to have fun, eat pizza, have ice cream, and eat chocolate. However, when you have a steady diet of restaurant and fast food, you are exposing yourself to foods that will *not* help any athlete excel! All good things in moderation! Enjoy dining out with friends and families, and take this time, even, to indulge during these meals. I just recommend, during competition weekend, keep it clean and balanced!

Summer Food Fun for Gymnasts

WHEN SUMMER IS HERE, there is no better time than now to take advantage of the fresh fruit and vegetables in our grocery stores. Gymnasts need adequate lean protein and lots of vitamin-rich fruits, veggies, and complex carbohydrates to get them through their workouts. Here are some of my own summer favorite recipes for healthy families to enjoy.

Note: The following are individual portions. You will need to double or triple the recipes to feed multiple people.

Power Protein and Fruit Parfait

1 cup honeydew or cantaloupe, cut into small cubes. Add **1/2 cup** kiwi slices. Mix into ½ **cup** organic Greek yogurt. Sprinkle with **2 tablespoons** crushed pecans and **2 tablespoons** coconut shreds.

Summer Turkey Salad

3 cups of mixed green salad. Add **4 ounces** of low-sodium turkey, and chop up **1 cup** red, yellow, and green peppers. Add **2 tablespoons** feta cheese or goat cheese, **1 tablespoon** apple cider vinegar, and **1 tablespoon** olive oil. Toss well.

Fruit and Veggie Kabobs On The Grill

Pre-soak 6-8 skewers in water for 10 minutes. Slice red bell peppers, a purple onion, mushrooms, zucchini, and pineapple chunks; alternate on the skewer. Make a marinade with ¼ **cup** olive oil, **1 teaspoon** fresh basil, **1 tablespoon** fresh basic *or* cilantro, **1 teaspoon** of salt, **1 teaspoon** of pepper, **1 clove** of fresh garlic chopped, 1 teaspoon of oregano, and **2 tablespoons** of fresh lemon juice. Coat onto the kabobs. Cook on the grill and enjoy. Eat 1-2 kabobs with ½ **cup** brown rice and **4-6 ounces** of your favorite lean protein, fish, tofu, or chicken.

Tuna Niçoise Salad

Place **3 ounces** of low-sodium albacore tuna over **3 cups** of spinach and kale mix. Add **4** fresh, raw asparagus spears, **1/2 cup** fresh green beans, **1** hardboiled egg white sliced, **4** cherry tomatoes, **2 tablespoons** black olives, and purple onion to taste. Use **1 tablespoon** red wine vinegar and **2 tablespoons** olive oil for dressing.

Grilled Mango Fish Tacos

Grill **6 ounces** of wild cod or wild whitefish with a dash of salt and pepper. Break up the fish and place in a large lettuce or Romaine lettuce leaf with the following mix of ingredients: **1/4 cup** chopped cilantro, **1/4 cup** purple onion, **1/4 cup** chopped mango, and **1/4 cup** chopped tomato. Mix all of these with **1/8 cup** of olive oil, and use as a "salsa" for the fish in the lettuce wrap. Serve with a cup of fresh melon or more mango!

Fiesta Grilled Salmon

Marinate **4 ounces** of wild salmon with olive oil, garlic, and lemon juice, plus a dash of salt and pepper before placing on the grill. Serve with ½ **cup** of the following mix: **1/4 cup** corn, **1/4 cup** brown rice, ½ **cup** chopped tomatoes, **1/4 cup** black beans, ¼ **cup** chopped purple onion, blended all together with fresh garlic and **2 tablespoons** olive oil.

Grilled Turkey Burger and Corn on the Cob

Grill **4 ounces** of organic ground turkey. Season with a pinch of feta cheese and fresh salsa, plus corn on the cob (organic if possible!). Serve with **2 cups** of spinach salad with **4** sliced strawberries, 2 tablespoons walnuts, and **2 tablespoons** each of olive oil and balsamic vinegar as salad dressing.

Side Cucumber Salad

4 plum tomatoes chopped, ¼ **cup** chopped purple onion, ½ **cup** finely chopped cucumbers. Blend all together with **2 tablespoons** red wine vinegar, **2 tablespoons** olive oil, and a **dash** of salt and pepper. Serve as a side dish with fresh fish or grilled chicken.

Summer Asian Salad

3 cups of spring mix salad, **4 ounces** of chicken, **6-8** tangerine or mandarin orange slices, ½ **cup** chopped green or bell peppers, **1 tablespoon** of sesame oil, **1 teaspoon** of olive oil, and **1 teaspoon** of balsamic vinegar. Add a sprinkle of almond slices.

Mahi-Mahi and Sweet Potatoes on the Grill

Marinate **4 ounces** of grilled mahi-mahi with **1 tablespoon** olive oil, lemon juice, black pepper, and garlic before grilling. Grill **1** corn on the cob with **1** teaspoon of coconut oil and dash of salt.

Eat with **4 ounces** of grilled sweet potato: Take a **4-ounce** sweet potato (you can make a larger amount, if cooking for more than one person); clean and slice well. Take a piece of foil large enough to wrap and make an envelope around the potatoes. Coat the foil with **1 tablespoons** olive oil, then add a layer of sweet potatoes and a **dash** of brown sugar then a dash of cinnamon. Add **1 more tablespoon** of olive oil. Cover and make a foil envelope, then poke holes in it, and place it on the grill. Grill until potatoes are soft and caramelized.

Betsy's Thoughts on Sports Drinks

TYPICALLY, IT DOESN'T take long for me to figure out why gymnasts' nutrition plans are going wrong. A few questions usually lead me to understand that they are probably eating too much processed food, fast food, *or* protein bars and sports drinks.

Now, before someone gets upset with me for "bad mouthing" sports drinks, please understand I do believe there is a time and place and a sport for them. However, gymnastics is not one of them. This is my opinion, based on the facts of the contents of these drinks, including the excessive sugar content, colorant, and abundant use of electrolytes. Let me explain.

While these supplements target the traditional endurance athlete, triathlete, or runner, gymnastics is a muscular endurance sport that requires quick bursts of energy. It is not a cardiovascular sport. A gymnast is never in constant movement for more than a minute and thirty seconds, as there are quite a few break times, and routines are generally under two minutes. Gymnastics is also performed in a moderately cool environment (summer months, of course, can be different, but in general, most gyms are either climate controlled or not excessively hot, other than occasional periods of the year).

Now that you know that gymnastics is primarily muscular endurance at work and not sustained cardio in heated environments, you will begin to understand there is really no need to supplement with sports drinks. Unless you are sweating profusely and doing 2-6 hours of hard cardio, running, jumping, cycling, or playing tennis in the hot sun, I do *not* recommend consuming energy bars *or* sports drinks.

When I look out onto a gymnastics floor, I see a lot of standing and waiting in line for a turn on the beam or waiting for a turn on the vault runway. Again, gymnastics is stop and go.

So why are so many gymnasts falling into the trap of drinking sports drinks?

They are quick, convenient, and marketed toward athletic performance, but they are not made for gymnasts and will not help performance. Here's why:

1. Too many supplemental minerals.

If you are eating a balanced meal plan rich in complex carbohydrates, fruits, and vegetables, drinking water, plus taking a multivitamin and not losing tons of fluid from excessive sweating, you should *not* be supplementing with extra iron, magnesium, potassium, niacin, riboflavin, vitamin C, and B-12. Taking these supplements excessively can throw off your body's natural balance of water, vitamins, and minerals. In addition, too much iron can constipate and lead to gastrointestinal issues, bloating, and sometimes diarrhea. This is one of the things many of my athletes complain about—being bloated! Power and protein bars and drinks will *not* help you in this area.

2. Too much sugar

A bottle of Gatorade contains 56 grams of sugar and 426 milligrams of sodium—that's an *enormous* amount of sugar and sodium! Sodium helps the body retain water, but gymnasts don't lose much water from sweat in workouts. Remember the bloating we discussed earlier? Sodium magnifies this problem. In addition, high-sodium foods are notoriously linked with high blood pressure and heart disease.

Gatorade's 56 grams of sugar more than doubles the recommended daily intake of sugar, which is 25 grams. Excessive sugar leads to corroding teeth, possible weight gain, and other debilitating diseases like diabetes, and it will not help your energy as a gymnast. Sugar gives an immediate lift, but 30-45 minutes into your workout, you will crash and become tired. For maximum performance, gymnasts only need WATER.

Sugar is not only a problem in sports drinks but also in energy bars. A traditional chocolate Power Bar contains 25 grams of sugar. This is comparable to a traditional candy bar of the same size, which ranges between 25-30 grams of sugar—your recommended daily amount of added sugar for the whole day!

Natural sugars found in fruits, vegetables, complex carbohydrates, and whole grains should be a gymnast's go-to energy source. For maximum performance, ingest these foods 1.5 to 2 hours before practice in the form of sweet potatoes, brown rice, oats, and fiber-rich fruits and veggies. The sugar in energy bars and Gatorade are excessive and unnecessary for athletes in anaerobic sports like gymnastics.

3. Too many hidden ingredients

Look at the ingredient packages of many energy bars and sports drinks. You will find a lot of names you can't pronounce. Look at a bottle of your favorite sports drink—why is it blue? The only edible food that should be blue is a berry or vegetable; anything else is artificial. Of course, some energy bars are better than others and claim to be natural. Choose carefully, and read the ingredients. A gymnast needs real whole foods and water. Too many man-made additives and preservatives are unhealthy.

4. Too many calories

There are simply too many calories in these drinks. Unused calories turn to stored energy, which becomes excess fat. You can get the same amount of energy from density-rich foods like apples, grapefruits, grapes, broccoli, spinach, kale, and many others at a lesser caloric intake. Be wise, and choose real, whole foods, complex carbohydrates like fruits and vegetables, and lots of water to power you to your maximum performance.

Unnecessary weight gain for *any person*, regardless of what sport they play, is not healthy. Put aside any stigmas related to gymnastics, body image, and body shaming. No physician will tell any person it is healthy to gain significant amounts of weight, if you are already within normal weight guidelines. If you are underweight, then the other four reasons in this article should steer you away from drinking sports drinks and steer you in the direction of eating healthier fats, proteins, complex carbs, and sugars in a safer more natural way.

5. And finally... too expensive!

If you consume sports drinks or protein bars every day, your wallet will take a hit. Gymnastics is already an expensive sport! Remember: many energy bars have just as much sugar as a candy bar, and a sports drink can have just as much as a Coke. It's more cost-effective to buy fruits and vegetables and snacks like nuts and rice cakes in bulk rather than á la carte from a snack machine. Take time to prepare by going grocery shopping with your week's plan of food in mind. Prepare snacks in Baggies for your gym bag so you don't hit up the snack machine when you are desperate.

Preparation is key. Take time to do this, and your body—and your gymnastics—will thank you!

How Much Protein?

ONE OF THE MOST prevalent questions I get from gymnasts and parents is: "How much protein do I need to repair my muscles after a practice?"

Protein repairs muscles after long, strenuous workouts. In general, an athlete (like a gymnast) should consume between 1.2 and 2 grams of *lean* protein per kilogram of body weight per day.

It is also important that gymnasts eat a significant amount of green vegetables, fruits, healthy fats, and complex carbohydrates to complete their diet regimes.

Here are my recommendations for the most superior proteins for a gymnast post-workout that will keep her/him light, fit, and looking and feeling their best:

Salmon

Wild salmon not only boasts huge amounts of omega fats for great brain, skin, and heart health, but it also packs 22.5 grams of protein per 4-ounce serving. Match this with a 3-ounce sweet potato and a cup of broccoli for an excellent post-training meal.

Eggs and egg whites

The simplest and purest form of protein is found in an egg white. Each egg white contains 3.6 grams of protein, so having 4 whites would equal around 14 grams of protein. My gymnasts match this with a half cup of protein-rich oatmeal for breakfast and some berries for a great start to the day.

Nuts and Nut Butters

Almond butter adds 5.8 grams of protein per 2 tablespoons. Add this to a couple of rice cakes or alongside an apple for a great pre-workout snack. Or, add 1/4 cup of nuts to any salad post-workout for healthy fats and protein punch.

Chicken

Chicken goes with anything! It adds 26.1 grams of protein per 4-ounce serving. Try chopping up chicken and adding to 1/2 cup quinoa and 1/2 cup finely shredded broccoli with 1 tablespoon each of olive oil and balsamic vinegar! Yum!

Edamame or tofu

Who says soy isn't a great non-meat protein? A cup of edamame is a great post-workout snack. Try 4 ounces of stir-fried tofu or edamame beans (33.2 grams protein per cup) with a cup of snow peas, onions, and 1/2 cup brown rice for a protein-filled post-workout meal! Drizzle with some low-sodium soy sauce for a bit of flavor. Look for organic, non-GMO brands, if possible.

Greek Yogurt

This yogurt has the highest amount of protein and lowest amount of sugar on the market. Try substituting Greek yogurt for sour cream on chicken tacos or on baked potatoes with a few tablespoons of salsa! A cup of Greek yogurt adds 20.4 grams of protein per serving.

Betsy's Healthy Snack Recommendations

EVER WONDER IF your snack contains all you need to power you through your training? Check out my recommendations for pre-workout fueling!

➤ Snack should include **complex carbohydrates** to refuel muscle glycogen. Complex carbs keep your blood sugar stable, so you don't "crash" halfway through your workout. Examples would be fiber-rich foods, oats, brown rice, sweet potatoes, whole grains, and beans.

➤ Snack should include a solid amount of **protein** to prepare for and repair muscle breakdown.

➤ Snack should include a moderate amount of **natural sugar** in the way of fruit, and a very small amount of **healthy fat,** to stave off hunger during or after workout.

➤ Snacks should always come with **hydration** in the form of water.

Some Snack Ideas?

Half a Banana Boat: Slice a banana down the middle, then cut it in half. Spread 1.5 tablespoons of natural almond or peanut butter onto the banana, then top with two tablespoons of raisins and a drizzle of honey.

Rice Cake Hummus Delight: On a whole-grain rice cake, spread two tablespoons of hummus, then top with four sliced cucumbers and a slice of tomato.

Fruit Kabobs and Nuts: Slide green grapes, blueberries, strawberry slices, and raspberries on toothpicks and eat them like kabobs. Enjoy with a side of 1/4-cup almonds or pistachios. Add string cheese for more protein. You can also freeze these kabobs!

Post-Workout Snacks:

Quick Lettuce Wrap: On a lettuce leaf, add three ounces of low-sodium tuna, two tablespoons of salsa, 1/2 cup of brown rice, and a slice of avocado.

Greek Yogurt and Oats: One cup of plain Greek yogurt blended with 2/3 cup of dry oats and one tablespoon of natural honey.

Edamame Protein Power: One cup of edamame beans, dried or fresh. Pair with a whole-grain rice cake, one tablespoon of light cream cheese, and a few strawberry slices on top.

Betsy's Portable Snacks for Gymnasts

IN THE CAR, at practice, need a quick after school snack? Gymnasts definitely should consistently be giving their bodies nutrient-dense foods throughout the day, to prepare for their long battles in the gym! Here are some of my favorite on-the-go snacks!

Peanut, Cashew, and Almond Butter Packets

No one wants to carry around a jar of almond butter. Check out these individual-portion packets, great for a pre-workout snack. Almond, peanut, and cashew butter are great sources of healthy fat, protein, and fiber!

Pistachios

These nuts are fun to eat and, like almonds, are loaded with healthy fat, protein, and fiber. Portion out 1/3 cup before a workout and get crackin'! Pair with an organic string cheese!

Rice Cakes

Whole grain rice cakes are quick and easy for a fast snack. Get creative with your rice cakes, and top with almond butter, apple butter, or cottage cheese and fruit.

Tuna

Get your protein fill-up with pouches of low-sodium tuna. Add some salsa for a quick meal, or eat on top of your rice cake!

Berries

Natural sugar at its finest. Pop these in your mouth before a workout for a great energy + antioxidant kick!

Dry-Roasted Edamame

Edamame are soy beans rich with protein and fiber. Eat them fresh or dry for a great energy snack!

Dry Oats

Oats are a great source of complex carbohydrates and ideal for giving you extended energy for long periods of time. Eat them with hot water for a delicious snack, or add them dry into your yogurt.

Dates

Dates are packed with natural sugars, fiber, and lots of vitamins and minerals. Check out the date bars recipe in this cookbook—they are amazing!

Dried Seaweed

Nature's only "real organic food," seaweed is a powerful snack, loaded with vitamin B for energy and iodine for proper gland function. This crunchy snack is an acquired taste, but the benefits far outweigh any negative you may taste! I recommend pairing it with something sweet, like a handful of dried cherries or berries.

Why Athletes Need Breakfast

IT'S 7 AM, you overslept, and you have to be out the door by 7:20. Will you have enough time to eat breakfast? Gymnasts *must* eat breakfast! I can't stress this enough!

But why do gymnasts need breakfast?

We burn most of our calories in the morning and afternoon, as we are at our job, attending school, working out, and just going about our lives! So, if you don't start your day off right, you will be setting yourself up for a crash later in the day, during your workout!

Imagine if you skip breakfast and are sitting in class, starving at 11 a.m. That could lead you to grab an unhealthy snack in the school vending machine, causing blood sugar to skyrocket, and setting you up for even more famine.

Then, at the lunch table, you are starving and pick some greasy, unhealthy foods like fries, pizza, processed pastries, or bagged chips. These will drain you of energy. By the time you head to practice, you will have missed breakfast calories and replaced them with foods void of protein, healthy calories, vitamins, and minerals, causing brain fog, lack of energy and lack of performance.

I know that is the worst-case scenario, but believe me, I see it very frequently in gymnasts. The best thing to do to avoid this problem is proper fueling upon waking.

Here are some time-saver breakfast recipes!

Pear Slices with Betsy's SuperPaste!

On Sunday night, make a paste that you can store in a plastic container:

1 sliced pear or apple

1/2 cup dry oats

2 cups creamy organic peanut butter

1/4 cup raisins

1 tablespoon chia seeds

1 tablespoon honey

Mix all of this together (take your time—it's a lot of "stuff!"). In the morning, scoop out two tablespoons, and place on pear or apple slices! Yum.

Overnight Steel-Cut Blueberry Oats

Place **1 cup** of dry, steel-cut oats in a large bowl. Add **2 cups** of almond milk, **1/4 cup** fresh blueberries, **1 tablespoon** honey or agave, **1 tablespoon** of chia seeds, and a **dash** of cinnamon. Cover with a plastic film after mixing together. Leave overnight. Unwrap in the morning for a yummy start to the day!

Avocado Cream Dream!

First, toast two slices of Ezekiel breadt. Then spread **1 tablespoon** cream cheese or goat cheese evenly over the toast, and place four very thin slices of avocado on top of the toast. For a protein extra, add two slices of smoked salmon! Delicious!

Homemade, Frozen Egg McNallys

If you are short on time in the morning, prepare five breakfast sandwiches on Sunday night and freeze them. How, you may ask?

1. Take five whole-grain English muffins and slice them in half. (If you can substitute other organic or Ezekiel English muffins go for it!)
2. Scramble up to eight organic egg whites and four whole eggs.
3. Slice up five thin slices of organic cheese.

4. Place a cheese slice on each open English muffin.
5. Top each muffin with egg mixture divided up into five portions.
6. Place the top of the muffin on the bottom and wrap these tightly with plastic wrap.
7. Pop in the freezer and pull them out as you need.
8. To warm them up, remove from plastic and microwave on each side 30 to 45 seconds, depending on your microwave.

Betsy's Healthy French Toast

Take two slices of Ezekiel or whole grain toast and dip into the following mixture:

Two egg whites

One whole egg

1 cup of almond milk

Dash of cinnamon

1 teaspoon coconut oil

Dip the bread into the mixture then cook on a pan with the teaspoon of coconut oil. After cooking, top with 1 more teaspoon of coconut oil and enjoy!

Nutrition and Confidence in Gymnastics: The Connection

I COME ACROSS a lot of gymnasts who are very, very talented but are lacking in one very *important* element that's holding them back from their goals: confidence.

As I work more and more with Doc Ali in our Tight Mind Tight Body Bootcamp Series, I see there is a direct correlation between confidence and developing physically strong and resilient gymnasts. One area in which some gymnasts are very far behind is proper nutritional intake, meal planning, and clean eating habits.

You see, there are foods that can boost a gymnast's confidence and enhance performance and mood, especially for very high-level gymnasts, but this is true all the way up from the tiniest level

How Is That Possible? Think About It.

Gymnastics uses brain intensity for *both* technical purposes and also mental toughness. If those two are lagging behind, then confidence will go down with it. A lack of confidence leads to questioning, holding back, balking, and not trusting one's own abilities.

Our sport is tough on the body! If someone is consistently sore, tired, or injured, they are going to eventually question their ability: "Maybe I can't jump high enough" Or, "Maybe my legs won't hold out for one more pass." This type of questioning can lead you to a tough spot.

Deficiency in any of these major organs and skeletal areas can tear down a gymnast's confidence: brain, bones, heart, skin, and muscles.

The food you eat has a direct response to your organs, whether positive or negative; the response will undoubtedly be there based on what you choose to put in your body.

Here are some tips for how you can improve your nutrition and confidence in order to take your gymnastics to the next level.

1. The Brain

The stronger mentally and more clear a gymnast is, the better her confidence will be at hitting those big, scary skills. Defy fear by eating healthy fat and powerful antioxidants. Healthy fat enhances mood and brain function. If you have "air head" or "fog brain" during a workout, it's going to be very challenging to flip that Yurchenko when your technique, timing, or thought processes are off. Here are some of my favorite foods to cultivate brain health:

Blueberries: some studies suggest this antioxidant is the most powerful brain food on the planet! Get in a half cup per day!

Pumpkin Seeds: these seeds have a boatload of healthy fat and brain-boosting minerals. Sprinkle them on salads and in yogurt!

Fish and fish oil: healthy omega fats are proven to help with memory and concentration. Eat at least two to three servings of fatty fish per week!

2. The Bones

Eating foods rich in vitamins and minerals support bone and joint health.

When a gymnast feels weak or has brittle bones, feeling secure enough to push their body through highly intense body movements can be challenging. If you think you can't do it, you probably won't!

Who wants to be worried about their next injury, torn muscle, or broken bone? The stronger your skeletal system and the more your bone density, the greater chance you can avoid injury. You can be confident in moving your body with the intensity it calls for when you are strong. Here are my favorite bone-healthy foods:

Seeds and beans: pumpkin, sesame, and chia seeds and soy beans are all loaded with calcium, zinc, manganese for lots of bone density. Add to salads, trail mixes, or eat plain.

Kale: a calcium powerhouse; load up on kale two to three cups per day in salads and in shakes.

Oranges: stocked with calcium and Vitamin C—double whammy! Have an orange pre-workout for an energy boost.

Sardines: okay, they are slimy and fishy, but they pack an amazing 320 milligrams of calcium per three ounces. Wow, you can't beat it! If you are tentative to try sardines, check out Lenny's Sardine Patties in the recipes section. Even my little finicky eater loves these patties.

3. The Heart

Eating foods rich in heart-healthy compounds increases cardiovascular output, which means better endurance and blood flow.

If you *know* you can get through your routine because it's "easy" by the last pass, you know you are taking care of your heart! The better your heart works, the better blood flow will go to aching muscles and joints and healing injuries. Here are my favorite heart-healthy foods for gymnasts:

Olive oil: add one or two tablespoons daily to salads with apple cider vinegar.

Avocados: loaded with potent vitamins, minerals, and healthy fats, avocado slices are great on a sandwich.

Tomatoes: known for their rich red color (from lycopene), tomatoes are one of the most powerful heart-healthy foods on the planet. Lycopene helps with blood flow and keeps cells strong.

4. The Skin

When a gymnast has a rip on her hands, it makes getting through a bar routine very challenging, painful, and can literally "rip" her from her confidence. The skin takes a lot of damage in this sport, from beam bites to enormous-size rips, food fungus, and toe tears. How can a gymnast perform with confidence when their skin is falling apart? Here are my favorite remedies for ailing skin:

Coconut oil: use in cooking, on skin, rips on hands, and skin irritations. It's anti-fungal and anti-viral, to fend off pesky fungus and infection.

Garlic: known for its allium and tumor fighting, ingest more garlic to fend off fungal infections like ringworm and athlete's foot.

Almonds, **walnuts**, and **sweet potatoes**: foods rich in Vitamin E and collagen (all are also loaded with Vitamin A to help brighten and repair damaged skin).

5. The Muscles

Soreness can cause a gymnast to second guess her ability to jump, punch, or grip. Inflammation is an issue with the modern American diet, which often includes a healthy dose of highly processed and sugar- and sodium-laden fast convenience foods. Get those processed sugars out and increase your confidence level by kicking soreness out of the gym!

There are many foods that deal with inflammation and can help you attack your event with confidence! Who wants to wonder if their legs are going to give up on them because they are so sore from yesterday's conditioning? My favorite remedies for soreness are:

Turmeric tea: some say it's better than over-the-counter anti-inflammatories. Have one cup of fresh turmeric tea daily.

Raspberries: packed with quercetin, a powerhouse against inflammation, raspberries are great for muscles and joints. Enjoy a cup a day for great benefits!

Coconut water: who needs a sports drink when coconut water has a natural blend of calcium, sodium, and potassium without the added sugars or colorants? Have a coconut water, soy protein, and fresh raspberry shake for an anti-inflammatory, bone-satisfying, post-workout snack!

Gymnast's Guide on How to Eat on Competition Day

A FEW WEEKS AGO, a coach contacted me about her athletes, who had bombed out at a recent competition. Her gymnasts had been lethargic and slow-moving on the morning of their competition.

After the meet, a parent mentioned that one of the girls had eaten sausage biscuits and hash browns for breakfast. Another only had a Pop-Tart. Both of these are highly-processed, fat-laden food options and offer virtually no nutritional value to an athlete.

How many times have you or one of your athletes lacked energy at a competition because of eating fast foods or the lack of a proper "pre-competition" meal?

I get this question frequently, from both parents and athletes. It has come to my attention that each kid is different, so it is challenging to create an exact plan for each athlete; however, there is a basic formula I like to follow when recommending a meal plan for the day of competition.

Normally, the issue is that most athletes will compete, at some point, during a time when their bodies aren't used to training. For instance, some kids who train normally in the evening may have early-morning competitions, while others who are used to training in the early morning or afternoon find themselves in evening competitions. This can really throw an athlete off in terms of food selections.

Here are some general guidelines when prepping for competition day:

1. *Do not* **eat a large meal filled with fat within an hour of competing.**

Foods such as French fries, hamburgers, fried meat, muffins, donuts, and pastries (yes, Pop-Tarts) are packed with unhealthy fats! These fats are slow-digesting, which means it takes your body a lot of energy to process them. This will slow up any athlete no matter how fit she is. After eating a high-fat meal, people are tired, slow, and lethargic. This is *not* the way to go into a competition! Stay away from sausage biscuits, gravy, whole eggs, burgers, and fries before a competition.

2. **Load up on complex carbohydrates the morning and evening before a competition.**

Complex carbs are slow-releasing sugars that will give an athlete sustained energy throughout the day. Unlike simple sugars, which will give a quick burst of energy then a quick decline. Here are some of my favorite options for slow-releasing sugar (complex carbs):

- ✓ Oatmeal with honey and a side of egg whites
- ✓ Whole grain toast with natural peanut butter
- ✓ If you are competing later in the day, brown rice, quinoa, green veggies, and sweet potatoes are my favorites for slow-releasing energy that will keep any athlete alert, energized, and fueled.

3. **Water consumption is crucial!**

Regardless of what time of day your athlete competes, water consumption both the day before and the morning of competition day are essential to athletic performance. Being properly hydrated is very important for cellular and muscular function, as well as muscle endurance.

I recommend athletes drink a *minimum* of 72 ounces of water per day. I have found that sometimes kids aren't finding the energy to get through their routines, and it has nothing to do with food and everything to do with their bodies being dehydrated, especially in warmer climates.

Make sure, the *day before* competition, your gymnast drinks a full 72 ounces!

4. Light meals and snacks an hour before competition.

I don't know many athletes who like to compete on a full stomach. For a quick burst of energy, a light snack about an hour to an hour and a half before competition time yields excellent results. This should be comprised of a simple sugar (natural), such as a fresh or dried fruit and nut, or whole-grain snack such as a rice cake with light dairy and/or fruit. My favorite choices are rice cakes with natural peanut butter or dried fruit, such as apricots or raisins and nuts, grapes, and apple slices. Avoid large amounts of fruit a few hours before competition, as this can also be disastrous to the gastro-intestinal system. Know your body and pick the foods that your body can tolerate!

5. When competing very early, gymnasts should avoid a huge breakfast and try to get in a lighter but nutrient-dense breakfast filled with complex carbs, fruits, and protein.

My favorite option would be a plain Greek yogurt with dry oats, honey, and berries blended into the yogurt. Here you have your complex carbs, protein, and simple sugars for an energy-filled morning.

Another great option would be an egg-white omelet with peppers and a little bit of cheese with a slice of whole grain toast and a small amount honey. Skip the butter and syrup for breakfast before a meet.

One more breakfast option would be a few scrambled egg whites and a half cup of oatmeal or a slice of whole-grain toast and two tablespoons of almond or peanut butter with a touch of honey.

6. Gymnasts should lightly snack between events on carrot sticks, nuts, dried edamame, coconut shreds, berries, or whole grain rice cakes.

These options provide simple, quick sources of energy. They should avoid large meals like sandwiches and burger—or useless processed snacks such as pretzels, chips or popcorn—during competition. These will make them feel tired, heavy, bloated, and gassy! Keep it light and nutrient-rich with apple slices, grapes, and organic cheese sticks.

7. For later-day competitions, always start with a good breakfast.

This should be comprised of complex carbs, such as oats and whole grains, or eggs and a little healthy fat, such as avocados or hummus. A decent-sized lunch should include plenty of protein, fruits, veggies, and a complex carbohydrate. Also, bring a protein-rich snack, such as a few tablespoons of cottage cheese or hummus with celery sticks and whole-grain crackers. *Never* eat fast food right before a competition, unless you want to bonk out before your last tumbling pass!

Consistency Is Key: More Tips on Food Timing

IMAGINE THIS SCENARIO: it's competition day, and you are set to compete at 8 AM! That's all good and well, but normally you are eating breakfast at 8 AM and headed to school at that time.

Your body is still waking up, and you aren't used to fueling yourself for a three- to four-hour workout—much less a competition.

Most gymnasts, and athletes in general, are creatures of habit. They eat certain meals at certain times, drink water at certain times, and go to the bathroom at certain times, so timing is crucial when preparing for actual competition-day eating.

Athletes often are thrown off by competition-day timing. If a meet happens too early, eating too much can lead to gastric distress. A meet that happens too late in the day can also lead to disturbance of schedule and meal timing.

I've written several articles on this topic and frequently am asked questions regarding meal timing and what to eat on competition day. Although every athlete is different, here are my suggestions and a review for competition-day eating for gymnasts.

1. Be consistent!

Consistency is key, and not just on competition day. Eating clean all of a sudden won't yield the best results. It's the choices over time and consistency in meal planning that will ultimately help you on competition day. Be sure you are adequately hydrating and fueling yourself with clean foods, protein, complex carbs, and healthy fats on the days leading to and on the day of your competition.

2. Eat complex carbohydrates.

Complex carbs are crucial to powering through long meets. That means you need to eat foods that sustain your blood sugar and give you consistent energy in the hours and days before a competition.

My favorites are quinoa, oatmeal, brown rice, Ezekiel bread, and sweet potatoes. Make sure you have a complex carb at least one to two and a half hours before you compete.

3. Drink water.

Often, I see athletes crash on competition day—not due to lack of food, but due to lack of water. Water makes up about 60% of our body, so, on a cellular level, if we aren't giving our cells proper water intake, our muscles and joints will suffer. Drink water throughout your competition day and the day before. Strive for 80-100 ounces of water per day.

4. Watch your "unhealthy" fat.

Fat takes a longer time to digest and can slow you down! I am all for eating healthy fat—gymnasts need healthy fats, omega-3s, other vegetable oils, and fish oils. However, eating foods heavy in animal fat or processed trans fats will slow you down and make you feel sluggish. I recommend healthy fats in the form of nuts, avocados, and coconut oil, if you would like to have fat a few hours before you compete.

Coconut oil is an MCT (Medium Chain Triglyceride) oil, which means the oil is used like a carbohydrate in your system, so it gives you energy to help you power through competition day.

One tablespoon on your sweet potato, on your oatmeal, or on whole-grain toast a couple of hours beforehand will help you remain energized. It will also help keep your brain functioning on a higher level.

5. Pack Snacks.

I highly recommend snacks that incorporate natural sugars and protein for quick bursts of energy. Here are some of my favorite "mid-competition" snacks:

- ✓ Raisins with a packet of almond butter, a teaspoon of honey, and a rice cake.
- ✓ Pomegranate seeds with an organic string cheese and a handful of almonds.
- ✓ Sunflower, pumpkin, or chia seeds with a handful of dried fruit, like dried cranberries or mangos, and a hard-boiled egg.
- ✓ Cucumber slices with walnuts and dates and a square of dark chocolate (80% cacao or more).

6. Avoid new foods on competition day.

Let's say, for instance, you have an early-morning competition and you don't want to eat a full meal before your meet. You have read and heard protein shakes are a great alternative to whole foods, however you are perhaps lactose intolerant, or sensitive to sugar alcohols or other additives that may be in the protein you choose. You spend the entire competition struggling with abdominal pain and gas! Be wise and choose foods that you know you can tolerate on competition day. Intuitive eating is crucial to establishing healthy food choices.

A great pre-competition meal is an egg white omelet with veggies scrambled. You could also try a few blackberries and a piece of Ezekiel, or whole grain toast with coconut oil. Of course, only eat this if you like it!

PART THREE

BETSY'S SUPERFOODS FOR GYMNASTS

Artichokes

I WANT YOU TO go outside of your comfortability zone and try this amazing veggie. My husband Mess first introduced these to me in France. His mother used to cook them, and he grew up eating them. I had never tried one in my whole life except, for in spinach and artichoke dip (maybe like most of you).

First, let's talk about the benefits and why they are great specifically for athletes and gymnasts:

1) Pre-Biotics and Fiber: Amazing for the digestive system. A lot of my athletes are severely lacking in fiber, pre- and probiotics to help with digestive function. Some kids are out of balance because of the excessive convenience and fast foods in their diets.

    Artichokes have pre-biotics in them, which help set the body up to absorb probiotics found in other foods. There is a ton of fiber in artichokes to help with proper elimination and digestive function.

2) Bone Density: Artichokes are loaded with vitamins and minerals like magnesium and phosphorus to help protect and keep bones strong. In addition to those two minerals, artichokes have calcium and even vitamin D! We all know the importance of strong bones for our athletes!

3) Brain Health: As we know, it's important for our brains to connect in order to make the right choices during long practices. The magnesium and phosphorus found in artichokes will only further help fire those neurons. There are studies to suggest a lack of phosphorus is connected with slower brain function.

4) *So* many other reasons, from high protein, folic acid, lowering "bad cholesterol" (LDL), and heart function. This veggie is 100% *in the grocery cart* for optimal health.

So, now, how in the heck do we eat these suckers?

They take a little preparation. You can bake, broil, boil, or steam them. For starters, you want to clean and brush them, slice off the ends, and spread open the artichoke. For beginners, I recommend steaming them in a steamer or boiling them in water that has a squeeze of lemon or apple cider vinegar and a little sea salt.

When you eat the artichoke, you peel off each leaf and scrape little part at the bottom, eating the tender part of the leaves. The most important part is the *heart*, which is at the bottom of the artichoke, the base of the stem. It's the "meat" of the veggie.

After cooking, pull away any remaining leaves. Scoop out the prickly final center "fur" to reveal the heart. Slice it and dip pieces into olive oil and balsamic vinegar for a delicious vitamin and mineral treat! *Enjoy* your artichokes!

Oh, if you want more great ideas like this or want me to create a plan for your gymnast, give me a holla. Yeah, I spend my days thinking about how to make our athletes healthier and create meal plans that do exactly that!

Green Olives

OKAY, AGAIN, MAYBE not one of the kids' favorites, but let me sell my case to you, because I believe green olives (despite some high sodium levels) are *critical* for gymnasts!

1) VITAMIN E!

First, one of the things we always discuss in my seminars is the very high stress level gymnasts put upon their skin, specifically beam bites, hand rips, athlete's feet (shall I continue?), *and* the *skin* is the biggest organ of the body. These stresses transmit all toxins, free radicals, and other environmental diseases to the skin and then to the organs...

There is 3.30 IU of vitamin E in one cup of green olives! That's an amazing punch for a vitamin that is notorious for skin strengthening and health.

2) MONOUNSATURATED FATS

Next, olives are an abundant source of healthy monounsaturated fat (no wonder those Mediterranean people have so many centenarians, people who live to be 100 years old!). This heart-healthy fat also helps to stop deadly blood clots, plus helps with inflammation for tired, sore joints, muscles, and bones. (We never hear about that from gymnasts! 😊) An anti-inflammatory diet is crucial for gymnasts.

3) MOOD ENHANCER

So, one of the *very, very first* responses I get from my athletes who start my meal plans (*and* their coaches and parents) is: "Oh my gosh! She is in such a good mood!"

Olives contain a significant amount of vitamin K, which is linked to brain health and serotonin boost... In addition, the healthy fats are linked to healthy cognitive brain function. We all know gymnastics is a very technical sport that needs *brain* and *body* power.

So, dabble in olives. (There are 42 mg of sodium in two green Castelvetrano olives.) I recommend sprinkling them on salads, or slicing and adding to pizza or sandwiches!

Give it a try. They are an amazing *superfood*!

(And, if you want a detailed meal plan that includes olives, come talk to me about my nutrition plans for gymnasts and gyms. This is what I do: I find and use the foods that make gymnasts stronger mentally and physically. It works!)

Sauerkraut

OKAY, OKAY, I KNOW you all thought I was absolutely bonkers when I said sardines are the most perfect food for a gymnast. (I stand by that still, by the way: I've received multiple videos of children eating them and positive texts. Ha-ha! I'm actually serious!)

But you are going to think I'm even more crazy when I tell you about another one of my favorite foods for gymnasts... *Sauerkraut*! (Yes! I'm going there!)

Here's the story...

The health and fitness world has recently become more enamored with an old-world practice of fermentation... As a matter of fact, fermenting foods (the act of converting carbs or sugars to organic acids or alcohol using yeast or bacteria) has been around for thousands of years.

Fermenting foods is also a natural way of preserving our food and, in effect, creating healthy bacteria for our guts...

One of the best foods to do this with is cabbage.... Or, in its fermented state = sauerkraut.

So, why do I love sauerkraut for gymnasts?

Because of the amazing probiotics, fiber, vitamins, and minerals, plus, specifically, these five reasons below....

1. PROBIOTICS: Help digestion, balance intestinal flora, help with constipation, bloating, and diarrhea; help gut function, and essentially help *mental* function. What I'm saying is the better your

intestinal track, the better you can absorb vitamins and minerals that help with all of the other functions of the body.

2.   BRAIN POWER: With a better functioning gut, concentration, nerves, and mental clarity will be affected. Everyone knows gymnastics is a technical and mental sport. Get your stomach in check and your brain will follow!

3.   IMMUNITY: Many studies prove that taking in healthy bacteria from fermented foods helps to keep the digestive track functioning properly, thus helping us absorb the immunity-fighting vitamins and minerals like zinc, vitamin C, and vitamin D, that cannot be absorbed properly without a healthy gut. Basically, sauerkraut can keep us healthy and fend off sickness.

4.   BONE HEALTH: Sauerkraut is one food that contains a high amount of vitamin K-2, which studies have shown helps to promote strong bones and bind calcium. One of the number-one questions I get about nutrition pertains to broken bones and injuries. Well, here ya go!

5.   It's YUMMY and FIBER-DENSE: Yes, it is! You may think your kids won't like it, and it does have a very pungent odor, but give it a try. In addition, the old saying that cabbage is like a *broom* that sweeps out your intestines is true. One thing I've seen, as I've traveled the country with my camps, is that gymnasts definitely don't get enough fiber; constipation and irritable bowel syndrome are more common than you think.

So, how do you eat it?

TIP: You have to pair it with a food that is a nice compliment to the strong taste.

Also, make sure, when you purchase your sauerkraut, that it contains just cabbage and salt. It will naturally ferment. OR you can make it on your own!

If you want more information on delicious foods for gymnasts or ones that can help your athletes stay healthy and push through injury, you should check out my Injury Prevention and Healing webinar on my website www.betsymcnally.com, under my webinar section! It's pretty useful information.

Zinc

AN IMPORTANT MINERAL for athletes would unquestionably be zinc. Where can we find it?

- ✓ Greens
- ✓ Chocolate
- ✓ Meat
- ✓ Legumes
- ✓ Beans

Are your athletes getting enough zinc in their diets? The RDA for zinc for women is 8mg per day.

Why do gymnasts specifically need zinc heading into competition season? Well, normally, competition season coincides with *flu season*!

Gymnasts and coaches travel a lot, so immunity is going to be compromised. Zinc not only helps to repair tissues of the body, but it is imperative for maintaining and preventing the *immune system* from breaking down!

Where can our athletes get zinc?

- ✓ Legumes (beans, chick peas, hummus!)
- ✓ Seeds, nuts, nut butters (sesame, pumpkin, cashews)
- ✓ Dark chocolate (Yum! Go for 70% cocoa or more, or cocoa powder)
- ✓ Shrimp and lobster (check your wallet first—lol)
- ✓ Meat (go with grass-fed or organic/non-antibiotic)
- ✓ Dairy and greens (yogurt and spinach)

Want a perfect pre-competition ZINC infused snack?

Try a **cup** of Greek yogurt sprinkled with pumpkin seeds and 1 **tablespoon** of dark cocoa powder and a **teaspoon** of honey! Zinc it up, my friends.

Oh, and if you want more pre-competition tips on how to calm nerves and eat lots of other healthy, serotonin-boosting foods, check out Doc Ali Arnold and me doing our Tight Mind Tight Body Bootcamps!

Sardines

I AM DECLARING The Sardine As The Most Perfect Food For A Gymnast!!

Before you turn your nose up to the idea (and I'm sure many 9-18-year-old little girls are going, "*Eeewwwwwww*," please listen to me plead with you on *why your gymnast* needs to be eating sardines. Because it is *quite simply*, the most perfect food for a developing gymnast.

1. Gymnastics is a BRAIN SPORT: In order to make awesome corrections while spinning in the air at the speed of light, your brain has to fire quick impulses to the body. Sardines have a *very high amount* of omega-3 fatty acids, both EPA and DHA, which have been clinically proven to help with brain function.

2. VITAMIN D: The most sought-after vitamin in the body, one that all gymnasts need to help with bone breakage, joints, and collagen production! We can only get this through the sun and some other foods, *sardines* being one of them... by the way...!

3. CALCIUM: Vitamin D cannot be absorbed without calcium, and sardines are *loaded* with calcium! 325-400 mg of calcium per serving! This is almost half of your daily needs!

4. Oh, back to the fatty acids: they also help with INFLAMMATION: Know any tired, sore gymnasts walking around your gym?

5. And how about 20 GRAMS of PROTEIN per serving: after a four-hour workout, those muscles are *beat.* No better food than a fishy friend like a sardine to take care of repair!!

6. MOOD: Know any cranky, moody gymnasts who need a lift in the gym? Sardines and their powerful fatty acids have shown to help enhance mood and serotonin release!

7. THEY ARE CHEAP: What? *Yes!* The world's most perfect gymnast food is *not expensive*!

Okay, naysayers. I hear you loud and clear! We love this idea *but we don't like the taste*. Check out Lenny's Sardine Patties in the cookbook, and give them another try!!

Plantains

I'M GONNA KEEP THIS short and sweet, but I really shouldn't, because of all the amazing benefits plantains can give to athletes!

You may think this is a fruit, and although the plantain is part of the banana family, it is actually a vegetable very similar to a potato. Plantains are filled with healthy fiber, potassium, and vitamin A, for great muscle function, plus skin and eye health.

I love plantains for gymnasts because of their abundance of potassium, which aids in muscle function and brain health. Plantains are also great for diabetics, because they help to maintain blood sugar. They are excellent for digestive and urinary tract health, as well.

If you suffer from kidney stones, you should check out plantains. Their fiber-dense content is also helpful with moving waste easily out of the system. They are much lower in sugar than a traditional banana and can be eaten raw or cooked.

Lastly, plantains provide an excellent source of vitamin C, to boost immunity, and vitamin B6, which gives us *energy*. A pre-workout shake with plantains is an excellent choice, as this veggie has been shown to release serotonin and elevate *mood*.

* ENERGY
* ELEVATED MOOD
* DIGESTIVE HEALTH.

Sounds like a winner to me!

Legumes

BEANS, BEANS, the musical fruit..., right? (Well, don't let that stop you!)

Edamame, lentils, chick peas, peanuts, peas, and black beans: what do all of these delicious foods have in common?

They are all legumes or vegetables/seeds that come from leguminous plant.

What else do they have in common? They are all on my list for *amazing foods for gymnasts!*

Here is why.

I just did a presentation on healing foods for gymnasts. A lot of the focus was on the importance of protein and specific vitamins and minerals for bone health. Do you know what food I kept touching on with respect to healing bones?

Legumes.

Legumes are loaded with manganese, folate, and protein, all three things essential to strong bones and forming connective tissue.

Manganese: This essential vitamin helps to form connective tissue and strengthen bones. It also helps with proper calcium absorption and helps to regulate the normal functioning of your brain and nervous system, as well. Something every gymnast can benefit from.

Folate: Folate is a B vitamin essential for the conversion of carbohydrates/energy metabolism. It's significant to the gymnast and other athletes because folate helps build bone marrow, red and white blood cells, and is essential during growth periods. Many gymnasts struggle with growing pains and injuries during puberty, so this is a nutrient you do not want to miss out on!

Protein: An average serving of edamame has a whopping 28.5 grams of protein! That is about the same amount as a serving of salmon or chicken! We all know that protein is the building block for our bones, muscles, and tendons. Protein is essential, especially during season training, when bodies get run down and fatigue sets in. Load up on legumes if you have a kid who isn't a big meat or fish fan.

So, how do we eat these delicious legumes? Here are a few ideas:

- ➢ Sprinkle on top of salads
- ➢ Have as a side dish with a tablespoon of olive oil and sea salt
- ➢ Roasted in the oven with a little olive oil and sea salt
- ➢ Hummus is an excellent and fun snack most gymnasts love!

Need a meal plan for your gymnast? You have found the right friend in me. Contact me for an individual meal plan or training program. I'll do all I can to help you! Or you can also catch my recorded webinar on healing foods. Go to www.betsymcnally.com and check out my foods for healing webinar!

Pickled Beets

BEETS, OR BEETROOT, are a plant root that can be boiled or eaten raw or pickled.

I get a lot of questions about beets, like whether they are healthy and should be eaten and how much?

My answer is *yes* to pickled beets! In moderation, they are a delicious energy source and packed with vitamins and minerals. Let's learn more!

Beets are high in antioxidants, hence their very rich, deep color, which has been used in food coloring for centuries. Betanin is a compound found within the beet that makes it red. By the way, beetroot juice helps reduce blood pressure in hypertensive people, did you know that?

From all the research I have seen and read, beets are extremely healthy, and pickling does in fact help to preserve the vitamins and minerals within the beet.

So, let me tell you why gymnasts and athletes should eat more beets!

1. Folate and Calcium dense: Folate and calcium are vitamins and minerals essential for developing strong bones. Bone breaks and stress fractures are extremely common in gymnastics, so this is an element essential for our athletes.

2. Natural sugar/carbohydrates and some protein: Believe it or not, there are actually almost 3 grams of protein in a cup of beets—not bad! The natural sugar of the beet is definitely an energy lifter. They are also sweet and delicious, a great alternative to any sugary or unnaturally processed snack! So, for *energy*, beets get an A!

3. Vitamin A and C: Beets are significantly high in both of these. When I hear that, I think *skin* and *immunity*—two things constantly being ravaged in gymnastics and many other sports. Look at the hands and feet of our athletes. Rips, beam bites, warts, you name it—the skin of gymnasts is often open and facing bacteria and fungus daily. That is why vitamin C is essential for immunity and vitamin A to keep skin strong and functioning. Skin is our largest organ. Let's keep it healthy!

4. Drawback—Sodium: 1 cup of sliced pickled beets has 490 mg of sodium, which is kind of high. However, when eaten with a clean, lower-sodium diet and in moderation, the benefits are worth it.

How do we eat them?

You can boil, bake and also sauté beets, but for a quick lift, I recommend chopping them and adding them to salads or even juicing them raw. Here is a great recipe for a delicious sweet and savory pickled beet salad your athlete will love:

3 cups spinach salad

1/2 cup chopped red beets

4 ounces grilled chicken, salmon or **1/2 cup** chick peas

1/2 cup sliced green pepper

1 ounce goat cheese or feta cheese

1 tablespoon walnut pieces

2 tablespoons olive oil and **1 tablespoon** balsamic vinegar mixed together as a dressing!

YUM!

Asparagus

ASPARAGUS IS ONE of my favorite foods for gymnasts and for women in general. It's a "sprout" food that, when eaten during its peak season, is best! You can find asparagus in purple, white, and green colors.

Here is why I love it for our gymnasts and ladies!

* Helps with PMS, bloating and depression. Asparagus is a natural diuretic, which means it can help with edema, menstrual bloating, and water retention. Studies have also proved that asparagus helps to fight depression and increase cognitive function, two things we struggle with during that "time of month." This can be helpful to our girls going through puberty and experiencing some of the less pleasant aspects of lovely "womanhood," during their four-hour battles at the gym!

* Asparagus is loaded with folate and vitamin B6 Vitamins. These two powerhouses together increase bone health, fight inflammation, and increase blood flow. Stronger bones, less soreness, and better cardiovascular health all get a *"check"* from this coach!

* This powerful sprout fights disease, cancer, and kills free radicals. Asparagus is packed with glutathione, a detoxifying compound that breaks down carcinogens and free radicals. Asparagus is rich in antioxidants and immunity boosting vitamin C to help keep our athletes healthy on a cellular level. Healthier kids = better athletes.

Any food that helps with PMS, makes stronger bones, and aids in immunity is a *huge winner.* Oh, don't mind that funky smell when you pee... There is a compound in asparagus that, when metabolized, leaves this delightful smell behind. But don't worry: the benefits far outweigh this stinky side effect.

Springtime is the right time to get your asparagus! Sautée it, bake it, chop it, and enjoy it in salads and side dishes!

Sweet Potato

AS A FORMER professional bodybuilder, I can tell you the one thing that got me through long, hard days of dieting were my daily indulgences with the sweet potato.

To me, they are the most perfect food for a gymnast or for any athlete, because of their many health benefits. There are so many, I could probably write a whole book on sweet potatoes, but I'm going to pick out the top reasons why I believe sweet potatoes are an essential staple in any gymnast's diet.

* **Energy**. What gymnast practices for four hours at a time? Most of them do! Sweet potatoes are "root tuber" vegetables, which means they store nutrients, vitamins, minerals, and water underground. Then, these nutrients are dispersed into the potato itself. They are loaded with vitamin A, C, and beta-carotene (which gives it its orange color) and other potent antioxidants. In addition, sweet potatoes help to maintain blood sugar, so they are the perfect carbohydrate for diabetics or athletes who need sustained energy for more than two hours. My athletes *always* have sweet potatoes in their meal plans, as they are "crash" proof! Maintaining consistent blood sugar is crucial to any four-hour practice!

* **Anti-Inflammatory**: All sweet potatoes are great, but if you can find the *purple* sweet potatoes, go for it. These magic potatoes are linked to the longevity of the people of Okinawa, who have the largest number of centenarians on the planet (the most people living past 100 years old on the face of the Earth!). The purple sweet potatoes have magic antioxidants called cyanidin and anthocyanin,

which are linked to helping inflammation and increasing immunity. You can find the purple varieties in most Asian supermarkets.

* **Brain Health.** I always say, gymnastics is a *brain sport*. In order to make the proper corrections and connect the difficult technical aspect of the sport, your brain must be operating on a very high level. Sweet potatoes are packed with potassium and magnesium, two minerals that are essential to proper brain functioning. Sweet potatoes also help to release the feel-good hormone, serotonin. In addition, many studies show magnesium has been linked to helping elevate mood, increase brain function, and ease depression symptoms.

These are just a *few* of the many reasons why sweet potatoes are the perfect addition to any gymnast's diet. Plus, they are simply delicious!

Bake them, toast and roast them, boil and mash! Add a little coconut oil for a buttery topping with a sprinkle of blood-stabilizing cinnamon for a lunch side dish! Have you tried the sweet potato fries that go with our avocado burger? *YUM*!

Bell Peppers

I LIKE TO CALL bell peppers the chameleon of antioxidants!

Why? Because bell peppers change colors as they ripen, from very early stages of green to yellow, orange, and red, and even into deep purple varieties.

As they ripen and change, they develop different powerful carotenoids or antioxidants that help with various issues in the body including:

- **Inflammation**: Go with the green, orange, and red for muscle joints, aches and pains!

- **Eyesight**: Red and orange peppers! Lutein and beta-carotene! Gymnasts need good eyes for all of the four events, specifically running toward the table!

- **Reflexes**: Bell peppers have a large amount of magnesium and potassium. As I have told you over and over again, brain health is crucial for our athletes! Connecting the brain to the body is essential for flight series, release moves, and landings!

- **Immunity**: Powerful amounts of Vitamin C in green and red bell peppers! Pair with protein-dense foods like chicken, non-GMO soy and fatty fish, to help develop collagen for bones and muscles! Keep your athlete healthy over the summer months!

- **Bone and Blood Health**: Go with green bell peppers here—lots of folate and vitamin K for cardiovascular health and bone density and good blood flow for healing and strength!

➢ **Skin Health**: I can't say it enough: gymnasts take a *beating* on their skin. *All* bell peppers are excellent for fending off the free radicals destroying skin cells with their amazing carotenoids and antioxidants.

How to eat them?

- ✓ Roasted
- ✓ Toasted
- ✓ Steamed
- ✓ Pan-sautéed in coconut oil
- ✓ Fresh and raw on top of salads or dipped into guacamole and hummus!

Get your peppers today

Oh, and if you need a meal plan or education for your athletes, don't hesitate to contact me: **Coach@betsymcnally.com!**

Quinoa

ORIGINALLY A SOUTH American food (from centuries ago), quinoa is a grain that gets its powerful components from its plant's seeds. It has become popular of late but has been around for centuries. So, why is quinoa great for our gymnasts specifically?

Protein. No other grain beats protein with a serious amount—8 grams of protein per only 100 grams! That's a *lot,* for a grain! Gymnasts need protein to repair tendons, muscles, and bones and to restore collagen.

High Vitamin and **Mineral Density.** Packed with calcium, magnesium, folate, and zinc—the four elements I believe most important for bone strength, density, brain function, and immunity!

Fiber. This seed has a large amount of fiber, whereas traditional rice and many breads are severely lacking! Improving the intestinal track is crucial for elimination of toxins and waste from the body.

Gluten-Free for the sensitive! A great replacement for gluten for those gymnasts and athletes who are intolerant, sensitive, or allergic to gluten.

What I love most about quinoa is the different, nutty flavor!

Honorable mention... Farro

SO, IN HONOR OF grains, have you checked out *farro*? Now, if you are wheat sensitive, this *may not* be for you, but farro packs a mean punch in terms of fiber, zinc, magnesium, and B vitamins—all the things I push for our gymnasts!

Read the stats and get some farro today. It's a much healthier alternative to white rice or other refined grains, in my opinion!

Here are the stats. One-fourth cup (47 grams) of organic, whole-grain farro contains:

Calories: 170

Carbs: 34 grams

Fat: 1 gram

Fiber: 5 grams

Protein: 6 grams

Vitamin B3 (niacin): 20% of the RDI

Magnesium: 15% of the RDI

Zinc: 15% of the RDI

Iron: 4% of the RDI

Farro is a nice change up from traditional rice, pasta, or potatoes. Have it as a side dish or add to green salads!

Berries and Tart Cherries

AN APPLE A DAY keeps the doctor away, right?

Well, for my athletes, I recommend a serving of berries a day to keep the doctor away! Berries are one of the top fruits I recommend for athletes. From the brain-enhancing benefits of the blueberry and the powerful anti-inflammatory properties of raspberries and strawberries to the powerful antioxidants and fiber found in blackberries!

They are also loaded with vitamin C and immunity-boosting compounds. Most kids and athletes love berries.

The greatest thing about berries is that, well, they are delicious! You will find them throughout this book in many recipes. Cooked, blended, or added as toppings, berries are your friend for so many reasons.

Tart cherries are also one of my favorite superfoods because of their powerful anti-inflammatory properties, as well as their ability to help release melatonin, the naturally occurring hormone that helps the sleeping process. Try a tart cherry juice shake before bed to relax and calm your body and to promote a restful sleep.

Dark Chocolate

YEP, I THINK you will be happy with this one. Dark chocolate is one of my top picks for gymnasts and athletes in general, for the many health benefits the it brings to the table.

Not only is it delicious (recommended dosage is one ounce per day) and packed with helpful antioxidants and minerals, it is a great mid-workout or pre-workout snack that elevates the release of serotonin to the brain. Here are my top reasons for choosing dark chocolate as your snack today.

> Dark chocolate contains compounds called flavonoids that increase the nitric oxide in the blood, making blood flow easier and releasing feel-good hormones called serotonin. It's a great option over processed, simple sugars that release a quick sugar high and make you quickly crash after. Stick with 70% cocoa or higher, when choosing your chocolate snack.

> Dark chocolate helps to raise the healthy HDL cholesterol in the body and has been proven in studies to help regulate blood pressure and fend off heart disease. Packed with anti-oxidants, iron, and magnesium, dark chocolate's health benefits are essential to any athlete's snack plan.

> The flavonoids have also been shown to help increase blood flow in skin (our biggest organ, and one of the most abused parts of a gymnast's body), provide a good caffeine boost, and help with blood flow to the brain, kicking off powerful neurotransmitters that help our athletes make those critical corrections during practice.

Pair dark chocolate with a handful of almonds or berries for a mid-workout energy boost.

➢ It's delicious, devoid of dairy and most kids like it.

Tip: Start with about 70% cocoa then slowly move your way all the way up to 90% for a massive antioxidant boost!

Get your chocolate today. (Do I hear cheers?) And check out our delicious chocolate recipes in the book, including our favorites: Gymnast's Dream Dark Chocolate Protein Pancake and our Homemade Double-Dark Chocolate Pudding.

Wild Salmon and Fatty Fish (Including Tuna, Trout, Sardines)

FATTY FISH IS definitely a gymnast superfood in my book!

Fatty fish is loaded with so much goodness, including omega-3 fatty acids, a healthy dose of protein, and vitamin D, a vitamin traditionally difficult to find in foods and that many are deficient in.

In our sport, there is a large number of athletes who suffer from stress fractures and other bone distress. Foods like salmon and sardines are both filled with Vitamin D and calcium.

Fatty fish helps with inflammation. That is probably the number one reason why I love it. Any foods that can help with inflammation and not *cause* it for an athlete are superfoods for me!

Fatty fish are also excellent for cardiovascular and heart health. So very important for our young athletes to have strong, functioning hearts and blood flow! Not only that, but studies have shown that people who eat more omega-3 fatty acids have a lower risk of developing depression. Fatty fish has also been linked to higher memory and cognitive function and elevated moods. All of these are essential for a gymnast, who needs a consistent diet of happy foods!

Final Note on Organic Products, Non-GMO and Farmed vs Wild Fish: I highly recommend eating *wild fish* whenever you get the opportunity to do so. Farmed fish are packed with colorants, antibiotics, and steroids, and they live in very close quarters. For happy gymnasts, try to get happy fish that are swimming along in the ocean, not stressed out in a netted-off area of the sea.

Do your best, of course. However, do get educated about farmed fish and the difference between organic, wild, and non-GMO products.

As a nutrition coach, I do not have an "agenda," per se, other than for my readers, gymnasts, clients to make the healthiest and most informed choices on the foods that they are putting in their body. Foods that are devoid of pesticides, antibiotics, steroids, and GMOs are my first choice, but again, there is a lot of research out there on both sides of all these issues. Be informed and aware of our food service industries, and make the most informed choices you can, when shopping.

We Thank You!

Garlic/Black Garlic

PROMOTES HEART HEALTH, alleviates tumor and fungal growth, provides significant antioxidants, and strengthens immunity... Sounds like a superfood to me! It's *garlic*!

Garlic has been around for *centuries* on many continents all over the world, both as a medicinal aid and food flavoring. Its strong allicin compound (that delightful sulfuric odor you smell) is responsible for all of the amazing health benefits listed above.

More recently, black garlic has become popular for its delicious taste and health benefits. You can find black garlic in specialty stores, as well as in Asian markets and online.

Black garlic is aged and placed in special heat and humidity conditions that range between 140- and 170-degrees Fahrenheit, for sixty to ninety days.

Through this process, the compounds are broken down and a chemical reaction happens. What remains is a delicious, sweet, caramel-tasting darker version of garlic.

This garlic can be used in soups, sauces, or eaten raw. Some say it tastes like candy!

The good news is that the "allicin" (the "good stuff" in the garlic) that helps provide its potent antioxidants, heart benefits, and anti-bacterial and tumor growth benefits is not lost during this process, *and* you can avoid that post dreaded garlic breath!

Some other great things and why our gymnasts can benefit:

➢ Heart and Cardiovascular Health: Stronger blood flow equals better heart and lung functioning= stronger athletes!
➢ Anti-Viral, Anti-Fungal, Anti-Tumor, and Anti-Bacterial: The immunity of our gymnasts is consistently put at risk in our gyms. No matter how clean we make our gyms, pesky viruses are abundant!

I recommend cooking with fresh garlic or black garlic one to two times a week.

Tip: After eating a garlic-rich meal, munch on fresh mint leaves to help offset the strong sulfuric compounds. *Or,* eat black garlic to avoid that issues! Worth a look into!

Betsy's Final Thoughts: Lifestyle Transformation and Empowerment: It's our Endgame!

A LOT OF PEOPLE ask me how I began coaching and teaching athletes in nutrition.

As a matter fact, the reason I started doing it is far different than the reason I'm doing it now. I first started because I had a passion for nutrition and fitness and to help people initially lose weight and feel better about themselves (non-athletes, regular people).

Then my mission transformed. I was doing it to help myself and my bodybuilding clients in a more extreme way as my bodybuilding career was taking off. That was too extreme and put me and my clients out of balance.

Then it was to help women achieve balance, battling a lot of my personal demons as I tried to help other over-dieted women conquer theirs...

Then it was to help gymnasts understand about processed foods, fueling for practice and competition, educating parents of athletes, and creating fun meals and clean eating regimes.

Now, it's an even bigger mission. And it's rooted in my childhood experience with food.

Recently, I went to a Tony Robbins conference, and I left in tears afterwards. Not tears of sadness, but tears of joy and revelation. The reason I work with athletes and gymnasts specifically is because I want to help build confidence and self-esteem. I want to build lifelong healthy people, so they can enjoy an amazing quality of life.

I have come to realize that through proper nutrition and fitness, we as coaches and parents can make better, more focused, and better fueled athletes, and in turn we can truly develop confident, strong young women and men. If we can give them the tools for healthy living, we are creating a foundation for a long and healthy life.

I also know that I have seen *first-hand* the extreme changes in athletes who eat clean. I can tell if a kid is eating clean just through their body language, energy, how they respond to coaching, and even their attitude. In order to do a sport like gymnastics, an athlete needs to be razor-sharp accurate in their thinking and mindset.

Processed foods and refined sugars, sodium, and trans fats cause cloudy brain and make athletes question themselves, especially in a sport like gymnastics, where fear is a big issue.

Who wants to question a big skill on a balance beam that they are afraid of? It's already hard enough to do the skill while hydrated and properly fueled. When you add on processed foods, you have a problem.

Through my education, books, and lectures, I want to help athletes realize that, through proper food choices, they will be able to have the confidence to perform at the highest level they desire and overcome fears.

In addition, the nutrition lessons I am teaching these athletes at a young age are lessons they will carry with them through life. And that is the most important thing to me.

It's not the gold medals. It's not the championships. Those are nice, of course. But the most important thing to me is that I am teaching kids healthy habits about nutrition, building strength and confidence, and loving themselves.

In closing, the benefit of teaching athletes about clean and healthy eating is that, when their confidence grows, their skill level increases and their performance improves.

So, ultimately, it all starts with the fuel they put into their body.

I don't do this because I love to talk about macro nutrients, calories, or protein content. None of that really is of huge interest to me. I want families and athletes to develop a lifelong relationship with healthy eating.

What *is* of interest is that kids and athletes see and feel the direct result of the food they put into their body in their performance and their personal success. It means empowering kids through education so that *they* can make the right choice.

In the end, they will choose their foods. We don't. If we can give them the tools, then they have the power to make the choice based on their own desires, not our own.

And that, my friends, is *EMPOWERMENT*.

Follow us on Instagram @GYMNACHEF!

ACKNOWLEDGMENTS

WE WOULD LIKE to thank several people and many others for inspiring us to make this book. First, we want to say thank you to our sweet children, who inspire us daily: Dalya, Lenny, and Ayden. We live for you and will continue to be inspired by you every day.

We want to thank Wanda Hernandez for inspiring us to write this book. Wanda is the mother of Olympic gold medalist, Laurie Hernandez. I was able to work with Laurie a couple of years back and spent a weekend cooking with her and her family. Wanda was very inspired by what Mess and I were doing to help athletes fuel themselves with proper nutrition. She said, "You two need to write a book!" So, we did, and here it is. She expressed that we had something really special, and I think she was right!

We want to thank my intern, Mary Grace Monzel, for helping us with the nutrition breakdowns; my go-to web and marketing girl, Shelby Cole, for creating my awesome website and store links; and Alexandria Bishop, for taking the amazing photos of Mess and me in our very own kitchen. And special thanks to Kathryn Galán, who edited the book and helped organize our recipes into clean, step-by-step instructions.

I want to thank my parents, Jim and Carolyn McNally, for supporting me and Mess throughout the process of writing the book. My parents have been particularly supportive during the past five years of our journey. I want to also thank my brother Jon McNally for supporting me in my career, reading my first book, and always offering feedback and support. Thank you Jon! You notice when people who care ask, give, and support. Shout out also goes to my aunt, Diana Tradar, who has also supported our journey and especially our children over the years. Mess would also like to thank his parents, Meriem and Abdelkrim Laouar.

Most importantly we would like to thank EVERY SINGLE PERSON who buys this book, all the gymnasts and families who have supported me and *us* on our journey, and everyone who has welcomed my mission in the gymnastics world.

All of the coaches who have hired me to come in and do Betsy Bootcamps, plus my clients and friends who have supported my mission. I could *not* have done this without all of you supporting me and pushing us to do this.

We want to help as many people as we can though this book and more to come, we are just getting started! Please feel free to contact Betsy at coach@betsymcnally.com or check out her website for more information on her programs. Also check out Mess at www.chefmess.com.

And finally, thanks to Kool and the Gang for providing the soundtrack to our kitchen.

Now..., *"Let's Celebrate Good Times, Come on!"*

ABOUT THE AUTHOR AND CHEF MESS

SINCE 2001, BETSY McNally Laouar has been a sought-out coach in the fitness world. She is a wife and mom of two boys, Lenny and Ayden (AKA Tomato), and stepmom to Dalya. A graduate of Michigan State University (Secondary English Education), she is an NSCA-certified personal trainer, certified sports nutritionist, professional bodybuilder, former gymnast, former high school teacher, level 7-10 gymnastics coach, and bestselling author of *Binges and Balance Beams*. Her book tells the story of a young, impressionable gymnast turned fitness competitor who overcame an eating disorder that plagued her later in life.

Betsy works professionally with gymnasts in nutrition and fitness through her online training programs, speaking engagements, and, most importantly, her traveling Betsy Bootcamps. She has worked with beginner level ones all the way up to Elites and Olympians. She specializes in promoting balance, positive and healthy body image, non-restrictive and performance nutrition, and strength training for gymnasts.

She also works with regular moms, athletes, and families in her online bootcamps, webinars, and training programs. She is available to come to your gym live, virtually or through web-based programming. For more information, check out www.betsymcnally.com or follow her on Facebook: www.facebook.com/BetsyMcNallyLaouarGymnastics/.

Follow us on Instagram @GYMNACHEF!

@betsy_mcnally_laouar

ଔଔଔଔଔଔ

BORN AND RAISED in Strasbourg, France, Mess Laouar's passion for cooking started at a very early age. After graduating culinary school, he worked in many diverse restaurants and caterers in France, including La Grande Motte, Montpellier, Strasbourg, and villages in Alsace and America. The chef specializes in the regional cooking of Alsace and is heavily influenced by the south of France, where he lived for almost a decade. He currently caters parties and events in and around the Cincinnati area and works with his wife, Betsy, in creating catered meals and camps for her athletes.

He is the proud papa of three children, Dalya, Lenny, and Ayden. You can book Mess to do a dinner or event here: www.chefmess.com.

Printed in Great Britain
by Amazon